Home Cooking

Volume Five

Made Possible
by

KitchenAid
FOR THE WAY IT'S MADE.

Courtesy of Wood-Mode

Home Cooking with Lauren Groveman: Volume Five © 2001
by Marjorie Poore Productions
Photography © 2001 by Alec Fatalevich

Editing: Barbara King

ISBN 0-9705973-1-2
Printed in Korea
10 9 8 7 6 5 4 3 2 1

MPP Books
363 14th Avenue, San Francisco, California 94118

Home Cooking

Volume Five

From the television series hosted by Lauren Groveman
Produced by Marjorie Poore Productions

Photography by Alec Fatalevich

Contents

Introduction

by Marjorie Poore

Every week, KitchenAid's *Home Cooking* television series, which appears on public television stations around the United States, showcases many of this country's best cookbooks and cookbook authors. This is a special season for us as we welcome our new host, Lauren Groveman, noted cooking instructor, cookbook author, and television personality.

With the abundance of American culinary talent and the millions of people eager to try new recipes and different ingredients, we seem to have an unending supply of interesting new cookbooks. The books take us on culinary adventures to many different countries, give us confidence to try new and unusual dishes, and reveal secrets from great chefs and restaurants.

When it comes to cookbooks, people seem to subscribe to the "make new friends, but keep the old" approach. New cookbooks are eagerly collected and tried, but the trusted and treasured ones—often stained and tattered—never lose their permanent position on the cookbook shelf and in the cook's heart.

At *Home Cooking,* we've also adopted that approach in choosing our guests. This season we brought back a number of our "trusted and treasured" guests. Jasper White, the godfather of New England cooking, returned with a wonderful new book, *50 Chowders,* and some delicious samplings from his fabulous Summer Shack restaurant in Cambridge, Massachusetts. Bruce Aidells, the "King of Sausage," came back with a comprehensive new work, *The Complete Meat Cookbook,* to answer all your questions about cooking with meat, especially the new meats of today with their lower fat content. The charming and talented Biba Caggiano, the West Coast's diva of Italian cooking, shared some of her beloved recipes from her birthplace, the Emilia-Romagna region of Italy, which she collected in her latest work, *Biba's Taste of Italy.* We had more delicious Italian offerings from Colman Andrews, editor of *Saveur* magazine and the recently published *Saveur Cooks Authentic Italian.* Rozanne Gold, author of

the highly acclaimed "1-2-3" cookbooks, which provide the ultimate antidote to long and intimidating lists of ingredients, once again dazzled us with the simplicity and beauty of her recipes, each of which contain just three ingredients. Ted Reader, griller extraordinaire, brought in a suitcase filled with stones, wood planks, and pine needles, accoutrements for a unique grilling experience that ushered in some unusual and wonderful flavors from his latest, *The Sticks and Stones Cookbook.* We were also pleased to have Jamie Purviance return for a shish-kabob extravaganza with more recipes from the all-comprehensive *Weber's Big Book of Grilling.* Then we were blessed with a visit from the ever-cheerful master chef, Fritz Sonnenschmidt, C.M.C., who spearheaded the publication of a new collection of recipes from some of this country's greatest chefs to benefit a student chef scholarship fund.

This season on *Home Cooking* introduced us to the inspired work and delightful personalities of some new friends in the culinary arts. Flo Braker, one of the best-known bakers in this country, showed us how to make some of her beautiful miniature pastries from her book *Sweet Miniatures.* Another baking expert, David Lebovitz, demonstrated some outrageously delicious offerings from his *Room for Dessert* book. Thai food expert Su-Mei Yu gave a mesmerizing demonstration of two dishes that included the fascinating history and traditions of Thai food. Next was a side trip to Ireland with Noel Cullen, C.M.C., who has nearly single-handedly taken Irish cooking out of the world's culinary shadows. From Vancouver, we sampled Rob Clark's extraordinary Pacific Northwest cooking from the restaurants Rain City Grill and C. Another Pacific Northwest culinary celebrity, Tom Douglas, showed us just how much more there is to the Seattle culinary scene than Starbuck's and salmon and even shared recipes for some of the best-sellers at his renowned restaurant, Etta's Seafood. Marvin Woods, a talented young chef, showed us what low-country cooking is all about—a blend of French, African, Spanish, and Caribbean cooking that puts gumbos and creoles on the world culinary map. We had some tastings from the creative and prolific author of single-subject cookbooks, Rick Rodgers, and his books *Simply Shrimp* and *On Rice*. Pam Anderson showed us how to cook like the pros with her *How to Cook without a Book*. She took us through the cooking techniques you need to know to have the freedom to open your refrigerator and start cooking with whatever's there. Cheryl Jamison proved she was *Born to Grill*, the title of her latest work, with an upscale grilled dinner of stuffed tenderloin and grilled portobellos. Author Diane Morgan showed us how to get through the most important and anticipated meal of the year with her book, *The Thanksgiving Table*, which contains the old-time favorites along with stylish variations. We also welcomed the delightful and gifted Michael Lomonaco, whose show we taped while he was still the executive chef at the world-famous Windows on the World restaurant at the top of the World Trade Center. (The restaurant was tragically destroyed in the September 11 attack. We are fortunate that Michael survived, though so many of his co-workers sadly did not.)

Finally, our host, Lauren Groveman, graciously showed us how to make wonderful and versatile challah dough from her award-winning book, *Lauren Groveman's Kitchen*.

Each of the recipes prepared in the programs are in this book. We hope they bring you many hours of pleasure in your kitchen.

Marjorie Poore
Producer

Chapter 1

STARTERS

Fried Flatbread Fritters (Gnocco Fritto Modenese)

Biba Caggiano/Reprinted from *Biba's Taste of Italy* (HarperCollins Publishers)

Makes about 25 fritters (serves 6 to 8)

Biba Caggiano is chef/owner of Biba's restaurant in Sacramento, California, and author of a number of outstanding Italian cookbooks. Made from a simple bread dough, these fritters puff up instantly as they cook; the results are a crisp golden treat, as light as air and impossible to resist.

1½ teaspoons active dry yeast
¾ cup milk, heated until lukewarm
Pinch of sugar
2 cups unbleached all-purpose flour
3 tablespoons unsalted butter, at room temperature
Olive oil or vegetable oil for deep-frying
Salt

In a small bowl, dissolve the yeast in the lukewarm milk with the sugar. Let it sit for 10 minutes.

To make the dough by hand, place the flour in a large bowl and, with your fingertips, rub the butter into the flour until the mixture has a crumbly consistency. Mound the mixture on a large wooden board or other work surface. With your fingers, make a round well in the center of the flour. Place the dissolved yeast in the well, and, with a fork, draw the flour, starting with the inside walls of the well, into the liquid. When all the flour has been incorporated, knead the dough for a few minutes, until smooth and pliable. Shape the dough into a ball.

To make the dough with a food processor, place the flour, butter, and dissolved yeast in a food processor fitted with a metal blade and pulse until the dough gathers loosely around the blade. Transfer the dough to a board or other work surface and knead it for a few minutes, until smooth and pliable. Shape the dough into a ball.

Lightly brush the inside of a large bowl with oil. Put the dough into the bowl, cover with plastic wrap, and let rise in a warm draft-free spot until doubled in bulk, about 1 hour.

Lightly flour a wooden board or other work surface. Punch down the dough and roll it all into a large thin rectangle. With a scalloped pastry wheel, cut the sheet of dough into 5-inch-wide strips, then cut the strips crosswise into rectangles. Lay the rectangles on a tray lined with parchment paper.

Heat 1 inch of oil in a wide, deep skillet over high heat. When the oil is very hot, slide 3 or 4 rectangles of dough at a time into the pan and fry until they are golden on the bottom, 20 to 30 seconds. Turn and fry the other side until golden. Transfer to paper towels to drain.

Arrange the fritters on a large warm serving plate, sprinkle lightly with salt, and serve hot.

Miang Khum ("Savory Bite")

Su-Mei Yu/Reprinted from *Cracking the Coconut* (William Morrow & Co.)

Serves 6

Su-Mei Yu, chef/owner of the acclaimed Saffron restaurant in San Diego, is the author of Cracking the Coconut, *a comprehensive book on Thai food filled with many delightful recipes such as this one. Khum means "one bite," an appropriate name for this Thai snack food, which makes an excellent appetizer.*

Sauce

1 tablespoon small dried shrimp
1 cup boiling water
1 (1-inch) chunk fresh ginger
½ teaspoon vegetable oil
1 teaspoon fermented shrimp paste or
   1 tablespoon red miso
1 (12-inch-square) fresh banana leaf, 3 fresh
   corn husks, or 3 dried corn husks, soaked in
   warm water until softened
1 stalk lemongrass, green parts and hard outer
   layers removed, minced
5 shallots, minced
2 tablespoons fish sauce (namm pla)
½ cup palm sugar or packed light brown sugar
½ cup roasted fresh grated coconut flakes
   (see Note)

Condiments

¼ cup small dried shrimp
½ cup unsalted peanuts, dry roasted
2 shallots, cut into ¼-inch dice
1 (2-inch) chunk fresh young ginger, peeled and
   cut into ¼-inch dice, rubbed with a couple of
   pinches of sea salt, allowed to sit, then rinsed
   and dried well
1 lime, unpeeled, cut into ¼-inch dice, and seeds
   removed
¾ cup roasted fresh coconut matchsticks
   (see Note)
4 to 5 fresh bird chiles or 2 to 3 serrano chiles,
   cut into tiny chunks (with seeds, for a spicy dish)

Wrappers

36 fresh mustard green leaves, stems trimmed, or
   15 to 20 cabbage leaves, cut into 36 (3-inch)
   circles with a biscuit cutter or paring knife

To make the sauce, in a small mixing bowl, combine the dried shrimp with the boiling water. Let sit until the water cools. Drain and pat dry with paper towels. Pound the softened shrimp in a mortar until it is the consistency of coarse cornmeal. Transfer to a small bowl and set aside.

Preheat the oven to 400 degrees F. Rub the ginger with the vegetable oil and wrap in aluminum foil. Wrap the shrimp paste or miso in the banana leaf, folding it over several times (or stack the corn husks and wrap them). Roast the ginger and banana leaf bundle for 20 minutes. Cool completely.

Peel and mince the ginger. Pound the ginger in the mortar until puréed. Add the lemongrass and pound to a paste. Scrape down the sides of the mortar with a spoon, add the shallots, and pound and blend. Add the softened, dried shrimp and pound and blend well. Add the cooled roasted shrimp paste and pound and blend well.

Transfer the mixture to a small saucepan. Add the fish sauce and palm sugar. Set over high heat and cook, stirring constantly with a wooden spoon, until the sugar is dissolved and the sauce is slightly thickened, 1 to 2 minutes. The sauce should have the consistency of honey. Add the roasted coconut flakes, stirring to combine. Transfer to a small bowl to cool.

To serve, put each condiment in a separate sauce bowl. Place the bowl of sauce and the bowl of chiles, together with serving spoons, in the center of a large platter. Arrange the mustard greens around them. Place one or two pieces of dried shrimp, roasted peanuts, shallots, ginger, and lime in the center of each leaf. Add a pinch of coconut matchsticks over them.

Have each guest carefully pick up a leaf and fold it into a pouch, top with fresh chiles or leave them out, depending on preference, and spoon a dollop of the sauce over it, then fold the leaf over the ingredients into a bundle and enjoy.

Note: Roasted fresh coconut flakes add a smoky-buttery flavor to a dish. Place 1 cup of grated coconut at a time in a large skillet over medium heat, shaking the pan and stirring until evenly browned. Cool completely before transferring to a jar with a tight lid or sealed plastic bag. Roasted grated coconut will keep in the refrigerator for several months.

Coconut matchsticks add texture to many Thai snack and salad recipes. They are good as toppings for desserts such as custards and ice cream and, like roasted grated coconut flakes, they keep for a long time in the refrigerator. To make them, after removing the dark outer skin, use a vegetable peeler to slice the coconut meat across the grain into paper-thin ribbons. Stack several ribbons and slice them crosswise into very thin matchsticks. Roast 1 cup of the matchsticks at a time in a large skillet over medium heat, shaking the pan and stirring until evenly browned. Cool completely before transferring to a jar with a tight lid or sealed plastic bag. Toasted coconut matchsticks will keep in the refrigerator for a couple of months.

Bruschetta (Grilled Bread with Olive Oil and Garlic)

Editors of *Saveur* Magazine/Reprinted from *Saveur Cooks Authentic Italian* (Chronicle Books)

Serves 2

Colman Andrews, renowned editor of Saveur *magazine, aptly describes authentic bruschetta as "glorious in its simplicity." He also answers the question—once and for all—about the right way to pronounce* bruschetta: *"bruce-ketta, not brew-shedda."*

2 thick slices of country-style Italian bread
1 clove garlic, peeled
Extra virgin olive oil
Salt and freshly ground black pepper

Grill bread over medium-hot coals (or under a broiler) until browned and slightly charred in places. Remove the bread slices from the grill, lightly rub with garlic to perfume the bread, then drizzle with extra virgin olive oil. Sprinkle with a little salt and pepper, if you like.

Sweet Corn Fritters

Jasper White/Reprinted from *50 Chowders* (Scribner & Son)

Makes about 24 small fritters (about 1½ inches in diameter)

These make a delicious accompaniment to a chowder dinner. It's worth the time to husk some fresh corn instead of using fresh or frozen.

2 large or 3 small ears of corn
1 small red bell pepper (4 ounces), cut into
  ¼-inch dice
3 tablespoons unsalted butter
1½ cups all-purpose flour
½ cup jonnycake meal or yellow cornmeal
1 tablespoon baking powder
1 teaspoon kosher or sea salt
½ teaspoon freshly ground black pepper
¼ teaspoon cayenne pepper
5 scallions, thinly sliced
3 large eggs, beaten
1 cup whole milk
Corn oil for deep-frying

Fill a 4-quart pot two-thirds full with lightly salted water and bring to a boil. Husk the corn and wipe away any corn silk sticking to the ears of corn. Drop the ears into the boiling water and cook until the corn is tender, 1 to 5 minutes, depending on the corn. Generally, the younger and fresher the corn is, the more quickly it will cook; I always take a little nibble to test for done- ness. Use a pair of tongs to remove the corn and let cool to room temperature. With a knife, cut the kernels from the cobs. You should have 1½ cups.

Combine the bell pepper and butter in a 5- to 6-inch skillet or sauté pan and simmer over low heat for about 5 minutes, until the pepper is ten- der. (This may seem like a lot of butter for the pepper, but the butter will serve as fat in the bat- ter.) Remove from the heat.

In a large mixing bowl, combine the flour, jonny- cake meal, baking powder, salt, black pepper, and cayenne and stir to mix well. Add the corn, the bell pepper with the butter, the scallions, eggs, and milk. Mix thoroughly, but do not overmix, or the fritters will be tough. Cover and refrigerate the batter for at least 1 hour. (The batter can be made as far as 6 hours in advance.)

Preheat the oven to 200 degrees F. Before you fry, check the consistency of the batter: It should be thick enough to hold its shape in a spoon. It will be thicker than most batters (such as muffin batter) and have a gritty texture. If necessary, the batter can be thickened by sprin- kling in a bit more flour, or thinned with a few drops of milk. In a deep heavy 8- to 10-inch saucepan, heat 3 inches of oil to 350 degrees F. Using 1 spoon to scoop out some batter and another to release the batter from the spoon, or using an ice cream scoop, drop 1 fritter (3 to 4 tablespoons of batter) in the hot oil and fry, turning it with tongs or a spoon so it cooks evenly, for about 2 minutes, until it is a deep golden brown. Remove it with a mesh or slotted spoon, giving it a little shake over the pan of oil to drain, and place it on a plate lined with paper towels to absorb the excess oil. Check the size: It should be about the size of a golf ball, no larger.

Then taste this test fritter, and adjust the seasoning and consistency of the batter if necessary. (Salt especially plays and important role in cornmeal-based breads, here enhancing the flavor of the corn and the cornmeal.)

Drop 5 to 6 fritters into the pan, leaving enough space for them to move freely. Cook for 2 to 3 minutes, until golden brown, turning them frequently, then remove, drain, and place on the plate with paper towels. Transfer to a baking sheet lined with paper towels and keep warm in the oven while you continue to fry the remaining batter; let the oil reheat to 350 degrees F between batches. Serve hot.

Maple-Planked Brie with Roasted Garlic and Peppers

Ted Reader and Kathleen Sloan/Reprinted from *The Sticks and Stones Cookbook* (Macmillan Canada)

Serves 8 to 10

Try this at your next dinner party and get ready for accolades. Who can resist melted Brie topped with slowly cooked sweet garlic and the added boost of flavor that comes from cooking it on a maple plank?

2 small (¼-pound) wheels Brie
½ cup plus 2 tablespoons olive oil
2 heads garlic, separated and peeled
2 scallions, finely chopped
1 red bell pepper, roasted, peeled, seeded, and finely chopped
2 tablespoons chopped fresh thyme
2 tablespoons balsamic vinegar
2 teaspoons coarsely ground black pepper
Salt
1 maple plank, soaked in water for at least 12 hours

Preheat grill to high.

With a sharp knife, scrape the rind off the top of each wheel of Brie to expose cheese. Set aside.

Heat ½ cup olive oil in a small sauté pan and add whole cloves of garlic. Reduce heat to medium and simmer garlic in oil until softened and beginning to color, about 20 minutes. Remove from the heat, and using slotted spoon, transfer garlic to a small bowl to cool. Reserve the garlic-flavored oil for another use. Mash garlic cloves using the back of a fork. Add scallions, red pepper, thyme, balsamic vinegar, 2 tablespoons olive oil, and black pepper. Season with salt to taste. Spread garlic and pepper mixture over the tops of the brie wheels.

Place soaked plank on the grill, close the lid, and bake for 10 minutes or until it begins to crackle and smoke. Being careful of smoke, open the lid and place cheeses on the plank. Close the lid and plank-bake for 10 to 12 minutes until the cheese begins to melt and bubble. Remove the planked cheese from the grill. Serve with slices of crusty bread, flatbread, or crudités.

Chapter 2

SIDEDISHES

Oven-Roasted Stuffed Vegetables (Verdure Ripiene al Forno)

Biba Caggiano/Reprinted from *Biba's Taste of Italy* (HarperCollins Publishers)

Serves 6

This Italian classic never goes out of style. The vegetables can be served warm with roasted meats or at room temperature as an antipasto.

3 small Japanese eggplant, ends trimmed and halved lengthwise
Salt
3 yellow onions, halved crosswise
3 firm but ripe tomatoes, halved and seeded
⅓ cup freshly grated Parmigiano-Reggiano
⅓ cup fresh bread crumbs
½ cup chopped flat-leaf parsley
2 cloves garlic, finely minced
½ to ⅔ cup extra virgin olive oil
Freshly grated black pepper to taste
3 red bell peppers, halved, cored, and seeded

With a tablespoon, scoop out and discard just a bit of the pulp from each eggplant half. Place the eggplant on a large platter and sprinkle generously with salt. Let stand for about 20 minutes to draw out the eggplant's bitter juices, then pat the eggplant dry with paper towels.

Meanwhile put the onions in a saucepan and cover with cold water. Bring to a gentle boil over medium heat and cook until the onions are barely tender to the touch, about 10 minutes. Remove the onions with a slotted spoon and place on paper towels to drain and cool.

Place the tomatoes cut side down on paper towels to drain.

Preheat the oven to 350 degrees F. Lightly grease a large baking pan.

Combine Parmigiano, bread crumbs, parsley, and garlic in a small bowl. Add about ¼ cup of the oil, season with salt and pepper, and mix well to combine. (The stuffing should be soft and moist; if necessary, add a bit more oil.) Arrange the vegetables in a baking dish. Place some of the stuffing in the cavities of the tomatoes, eggplant, and peppers, and scatter the remainder over the onions. Drizzle with a bit of additional olive oil. (The dish can be prepared up to this point several hours ahead and set aside, covered, at room temperature.)

Place the pan on the center rack of the oven and bake until the vegetables are soft and a nice color, about 1 hour. Serve hot or at room temperature.

Table setting by Vietri.

Gratin of Fennel and Tomato

Diane Morgan/Reprinted from *The Thanksgiving Table* (Chronicle Books)

Serves 10

While this recipe comes from Diane Morgan's wonderful Thanksgiving cookbook, it's a side dish that can be served any time of the year since it partners so well with different meats, poultry, or seafood. It can be made in advance, refrigerated, and cooked just before serving.

³/₄ cup dried bread crumbs
5 tablespoons olive oil
3 cloves garlic, minced
1 large yellow onion (about 12 ounces), halved, and cut into ¹/₄-inch slices
6 fennel bulbs, trimmed of stalks, halved, cored, and cut into ¹/₄-inch slices
1 (-ounce) can diced tomatoes, drained
1 teaspoon salt
Freshly ground pepper
³/₄ cup (3 ounces) grated Parmesan cheese, preferably Parmigiano-Reggiano
Minced zest of 1 lemon

In an 8-inch skillet over medium-high heat, toast the bread crumbs, stirring constantly, until golden brown, about 2 minutes. Set aside to cool.

In a 12-inch sauté pan, heat the oil over medium heat, and swirl to coat the pan. Sauté the garlic and onion until soft, but not brown, about 3 minutes. Add the fennel and continue sautéing, stirring frequently, until the fennel has softened and is beginning to brown, about 5 minutes. Add the tomatoes, salt, and pepper to taste. Lower the heat to medium-low and cook, stirring frequently, for 5 minutes longer. Transfer to a shallow oven-to-table casserole or gratin dish.

Preheat the oven to 425 degrees F. In a medium bowl, combine the bread crumbs, Parmesan, and lemon zest. Sprinkle evenly over the fennel mixture. (The gratin can be made up to this point 6 to 8 hours ahead. Cover, and set aside at room temperature.)

Bake the gratin until heated through and the topping is crisp, about 20 minutes. Serve immediately.

Plank-Roasted Root Vegetables

Ted Reader and Kathleen Sloan/Reprinted from *The Sticks and Stones Cookbook* (Macmillan Canada)

Serves 8

Cooking root vegetables on a cedar plank adds a whole new dimension of smokiness and flavor to them. This dish can be made with an indoor oven or grilled outdoors.

1 small butternut squash, peeled and seeded
2 large carrots, peeled
2 large parsnips, peeled
1 small celery root, peeled
1 large onion, peeled and cut into 12 wedges
12 cloves garlic
2 tablespoons coarsely ground black pepper
¼ cup malt vinegar
3 tablespoons vegetable oil
Salt and freshly grated nutmeg
1 cedar plank, soaked in water for at least 12 hours
Water, apple cider, or juice as needed

Preheat oven to 425 degrees F.

Cut the squash, carrots, parsnips, and celery root into 2-inch chunks. In a large bowl, toss together onions, garlic, squash, carrots, parsnips, celery root, pepper, vinegar, and oil. Season liberally with salt and nutmeg.

Place the plank in a roasting pan large enough to hold it loosely and add enough water, cider, or juice to float the plank. Place the pan with the plank in the oven for 10 minutes. Place the vegetables on the plank and roast for 45 to 60 minutes, or until the vegetables are tender and slightly charred. Season again if necessary and serve.

Wilted Fancy Lettuces

Cheryl Jamison and Bill Jamison/Reprinted from *Born to Grill* (Harvard Common Press)

Serves 4 to 6

If you haven't tried grilling lettuces, it's a real treat. Besides tasting great, the combination of endive, with its pale green color, and radicchio, with its deep burgundy tones, makes a beautiful presentation.

Vinaigrette Marinade
3 tablespoons extra virgin olive oil
1 tablespoon red wine vinegar
1 plump clove garlic, minced
1/4 teaspoon sugar (optional)

4 small to medium heads endive, halved vertically
2 small to medium heads radicchio, quartered
   through the stem end

Prepare the vinaigrette, whisking together the ingredients in a small bowl. Place the endive and radicchio in a plastic bag or bowl and pour the marinade over them. Let the lettuces sit at room temperature for 15 to 30 minutes, turning occasionally.

Fire up the grill, bringing the temperature to medium (4 to 5 seconds with the hand test).

Drain the endive and radicchio, discarding the marinade.

Grill the lettuces, uncovered, over medium heat for 8 to 12 minutes, depending on size, turning once, until soft with a few brown edges. If grilling covered, cook 7 to 10 minutes, turning once midway.

Serve the lettuces hot or at room temperature. The endive and radicchio pair well with a hearty steak and can be cooked at the same time on the medium heat of a two-level fire.

Steamed/Sautéed Vegetables

Pam Anderson/Reprinted from *How to Cook without a Book* (Bantam Doubleday Dell Publishers)

Serves 4

This recipe contains an interesting technique in which vegetables are initially steamed and as the water cooks away, the lid is removed and they start to sauté. While the choice of vegetables is left up to the cook, try to select ones that have similar cooking times.

⅓ cup water
1 tablespoon fat (extra virgin olive oil, vegetable oil, butter, or bacon fat)
½ teaspoon salt
1 pound prepared vegetable

Optional Aromatics
½ small onion, sliced thin, or 2 medium garlic cloves, minced
Optional spices, dried/fresh herbs, and/or flavorings
Ground black pepper

Bring the water, fat, salt, and vegetable, along with optional aromatics, to a boil in a Dutch oven or a large deep skillet. Cover and steam over medium-high heat until the vegetable is brightly colored and just tender, 5 to 10 minutes, depending on the vegetable size.

Remove the lid and continue to cook until the liquid evaporates, 1 to 2 minutes longer, adding optional fresh herbs and/or other flavorings at this point. Sauté to intensify flavors, 1 to 2 minutes longer. Adjust seasonings, including pepper to taste, and serve.

Sweet-and-Sour Onions with Balsamic Vinegar (Cipolline in Agrodolce)

Biba Caggiano/Reprinted from *Biba's Taste of Italy* (HarperCollins Publishers)

Serves 4

Leave it to the Italians to come up with such an inviting side dish using small white onions coated with a sweet balsamic glaze. It goes well with any roasted or grilled meat or poultry.

2 pounds small white boiling onions
3 tablespoons unsalted butter
1 cup dry white wine, plus more if needed
¼ cup packed dark brown sugar
2 tablespoons red wine vinegar
3 tablespoons good-quality balsamic vinegar
Salt to taste

To peel the onions, cut an X in the root end of each one. Bring a large pot of water to a boil over high heat, add the onions, and cook for 2 minutes. Drain the onions and drop them into a large bowl of ice water to stop cooking. Drain again. Peel the onions and remove the dangling "tails." (The onions can be prepared up to this point several hours or a day ahead. Put them in a bowl between layers of paper towels, cover, and refrigerate until ready to use.)

Melt the butter in a large skillet over medium heat. When the butter begins to foam, add the onions and stir for a minute or two, then add the wine. As soon as the wine comes to a boil, reduce the heat to low, cover the skillet, and simmer gently for 30 to 35 minutes, adding a bit more wine or water if the onions start to stick to the bottom of the skillet. When the onions are tender but still a bit firm to the bite, remove the lid, raise the heat to high, and cook, stirring, until all the liquid has evaporated.

Add the brown sugar, red wine vinegar, and balsamic vinegar and season with salt. Cook, stirring, until the onions are golden and the pan juices reduce to a thick brown glaze that coats the onions. Taste, adjust the seasoning, and serve hot.

Bread Stuffing with Apples, Bacon, and Caramelized Onions

Diane Morgan/Reprinted from *The Thanksgiving Table* (Chronicle Books)

Serves 12

You may want to make this delicious stuffing even before Thanksgiving rolls around. Note the trick of using a bit of sugar to speed up the process of caramelizing onions, which can be very time consuming.

1 tablespoon unsalted butter, softened
10 cups unseasoned dry bread cubes
8 ounces bacon, cut into 1-inch pieces
1¼ pounds pearl onions, peeled and halved
1 tablespoon sugar
2 Granny Smith apples (about 6 ounces each), peeled, cored, and cut into ½-inch dice
3 large stalks celery, chopped
⅔ cup minced fresh parsley
1 tablespoon fresh thyme leaves
1 tablespoon minced fresh sage
1 teaspoon salt
Freshly ground pepper
3 large eggs, lightly beaten
4 cups homemade chicken stock, or canned low-sodium chicken broth

Preheat the oven to 350 degrees F. Coat a deep 9 by 13-inch baking pan with the butter. Place the bread cubes in a very large mixing bowl. In a 10-inch sauté pan, cook the bacon over medium heat until crisp. Drain and add to the bread in the bowl. Remove all but 2 tablespoons of bacon fat from the pan, reserving the extra. Add the onions to the pan and sauté over medium-high heat, stirring frequently, until soft and lightly browned, about 5 minutes. Sprinkle the sugar over the onions and sauté, stirring constantly, until the onions turn golden and the edges caramelize, about 3 to 5 minutes. Add to the bread in the bowl.

Return the pan to medium heat, add 2 tablespoons of the reserved bacon fat and swirl to coat the pan. Add the apples and celery and sauté, stirring frequently, until softened, about 5 to 7 minutes. Add the parsley, thyme, sage, salt, and a few grinds of pepper, and sauté 1 minute longer. Add this mixture to the bread cubes, and stir to combine. Add the beaten eggs and stock to the bowl, and mix well. Place the stuffing in the prepared pan and bake, uncovered, until the top is lightly browned and crusty, about 1 hour.

If you have room in your oven, bake the stuffing while the turkey is roasting. Otherwise, bake it beforehand and reheat it once the turkey is out.

Crispy Sesame Rice Cakes

Tom Douglas/Reprinted from *Tom Douglas' Seattle Kitchen* (William Morrow & Co.)

Serves 6

This is an adventurous side dish that juxtaposes both creamy and crunchy textures and mild and spicy flavorings. It's great for entertaining since you can make the rice a day or two in advance and panfry just before serving.

2 cups Japanese short-grain rice
2½ cups cold water
⅔ cup sliced scallions (about 3), white and
  green parts
4 teaspoons peeled and grated fresh ginger
4 teaspoons rice wine vinegar
1 tablespoon toasted sesame seeds, preferably
  a combination of black and white sesame seeds
1 tablespoon Asian fish sauce
1 teaspoon sesame oil
1 teaspoon fresh lime juice
1 teaspoon sambal olek or other Asian chile
  paste, or more to taste
Peanut oil for panfrying, about ¼ cup

Place the raw rice in a fine-mesh strainer and rinse under cold running water until the water runs clear. In a small pot, combine the rice and water. Bring to a boil, then reduce the heat to a simmer, cover, and cook for 20 minutes. Remove from the heat and let sit, covered, for 5 minutes.

In a bowl, combine the cooked rice with the scallions, ginger, vinegar, sesame seeds, fish sauce, sesame oil, lime juice, and sambal olek. Spray a jelly-roll pan (a 14 by 10-inch baking pan with a 1-inch rim) with nonstick vegetable spray or grease it with a little peanut oil. Press the rice into the pan with a rubber spatula. This amount of rice will not fill the whole pan. Just be sure to press the rice into an even ¾-inch-thick layer. Chill the rice, covered with plastic wrap, for at least 1 hour. When chilled, cut into 6 squares.

Heat the peanut oil in a large nonstick sauté pan over medium-high heat. Panfry the rice cakes on both sides until golden brown, about 3 minutes per side. Drain on paper towels and serve immediately.

Note: You can cover the filled baking pan with plastic wrap and refrigerate for 1 to 2 days before cutting the rice cakes into squares and panfrying them.

Carrots in Orange Sauce

Noel Cullen/ Reprinted from *Elegant Irish Cooking* (Lebhar-Friedman Books)

Serves 4

This is a wonderful and simple way to dress up cooked carrots from Noel Cullen, one of America's leading certified master chefs.

½ cup orange juice
1 teaspoon orange zest
1 teaspoon lemon juice
1 teaspoon cornstarch
2 medium carrots, peeled and sliced
½ teaspoon salt
½ teaspoon granulated sugar

Place the orange juice in a medium saucepan. Bring to a boil. Add the orange zest and lemon juice.

Dissolve the cornstarch in a tablespoon of cold water. Add to the orange juice mixture, stir until the sauce thickens.

Gently boil the carrots in water seasoned with salt and sugar until crisp-tender. Shock in ice water.

Mix carrots into sauce. Reheat. Serve hot.

Padd Thai Bann Gog ("Bangkok-Style Padd Thai")

Su-Mei Yu/Reprinted from *Cracking the Coconut* (William Morrow & Co.)

Serves 1

Padd Thai vendors all over Bangkok take great pride in preparing this savory noodle dish, which has grown in popularity here in America as more and more people get to know Thai food. As Sue-Mei explains, "It takes a lot of practice to make it good, and perseverance to make it perfect."

¼ cup vegetable oil
3 large cloves garlic, minced
2 to 3 ounces dried wide rice noodles, softened in warm water and loosely packed (about 2 cups)
1 cup water (or as needed)
2 tablespoons rice vinegar or cider vinegar
1 teaspoon fish sauce (namm pla)
⅓ cup diced fried tofu
1 tablespoon dried baby shrimp
1 tablespoon salted Tien Jing cabbage or salt-packed capers, rinsed and dried
2 tablespoons unsalted peanuts, dry roasted and ground
½ teaspoon Roasted Dried Chile Powder (recipe follows)
1 tablespoon sugar
¼ pound fresh bean sprouts (1 cup)
10 to 12 blades Chinese chives or 2 whole scallions, cut into 1-inch lengths
1 large egg

Garnishes and Accompaniments
2 ounces fresh bean sprouts (½ cup)
3 to 4 blades Chinese chives or 1 whole scallion
¼ young banana blossom or ½ head Belgian endive, sliced into 2 to 3 wedges
1 lime, sliced into wedges

Heat a 12-inch skillet or flat-bottomed wok over high heat for 1 to 2 minutes. To test for readiness, put your hand 2 to 3 inches above the skillet: If you can feel the heat, the skillet is hot enough. Add 3 tablespoons of the oil and the garlic and cook, stirring to prevent burning, until the garlic is golden. Lower the heat to medium, add the noodles, and cook, stirring with 2 spatulas to separate the noodles. If the noodles start to clump, lower the heat and add 1 tablespoon water, stirring and tossing. Continue to add water 1 tablespoon at a time if necessary. Stir-fry until the noodles are cooked but not soggy. Add the vinegar, fish sauce, tofu, dried shrimp, and salted cabbage and continue to cook, stirring for 1 minute. Sprinkle the peanuts, chile powder, and sugar on top of the noodle mixture and stir to mix, then quickly mix in the bean sprouts and Chinese chives. Push the noodle mixture to one side of the skillet. Break the egg directly into the oil and scramble it lightly. When the egg begins to set, push the noodle mixture back on top of the egg, then slide the noodle mixture onto a serving platter. Garnish with bean sprouts, Chinese chives, banana blossom, and lime wedges. Serve immediately.

Roasted Dried Chile Powder
Makes about ½ cup

**1 cup dried de árbol or japonés chiles, for mild
to medium-spicy powder, or 1 cup dried chiltepín
chiles for an extremely spicy powder, stems
removed**
Sea salt

In a 12-inch skillet, dry-roast the dried chiles over
medium heat, shaking the skillet or tossing and
stirring with a wooden spatula to ensure even
heating, until blackened. To cut down the fumes,
add a pinch of sea salt to the skillet. Transfer to
a plate to cool completely.

In a food processor with a steel blade, add the
chiles, and process until they turn to a powder.
Let the powder settle in the machine for a minute
or two; even so, when you remove the food processor lid, do so at arm's length, and do not inhale
the powder. Carefully transfer the powder to a
glass jar, seal with a tight-fitting lid, and store
at room temperature for up to a year. Remember
that the chile powder will be slightly salty, so add
salt accordingly in recipes.

Chapter 3

SOUPS
SALADS
&
BREADS

Vegetable Gumbo

Marvin Woods/Reprinted from *The New Low-Country Cooking* (William Morrow & Co.)

Serves 4 to 6

Here's a wonderful use of Creole sauce, which can be made ahead of time and kept refrigerated for up to a week or frozen for several months. Okra comes from Africa, where it was brought to America with the slave trade in the eighteenth century.

2 tablespoons vegetable oil
2 cups thinly sliced fresh okra
2 stalks celery, diced
1 green bell pepper, seeded and chopped
1 cup fresh or thawed frozen corn kernels
1/2 onion, chopped
3 cups Creole Sauce (page 94)
1 tablespoon finely chopped fresh thyme leaves
1 tablespoon finely chopped fresh rosemary leaves
1/2 cup chopped fresh or drained canned tomatoes
Salt and freshly ground black pepper, or Marv's
   Bay Spice (recipe follows), to taste
Hot cooked white rice

In a large soup pot, heat the oil over medium heat. Add the okra, celery, green pepper, corn, and onion. Cook, stirring occasionally, until the vegetables start to soften, 5 to 10 minutes. Add the Creole Sauce. Bring the mixture to a boil. Reduce the heat and let simmer for 5 minutes. Add the herbs and tomatoes and simmer 5 to 10 minutes more. Taste and check the seasoning, adding salt and pepper or Marv's Bay Spice, if needed. Serve over rice.

Marv's Bay Spice
Makes about 1 1/2 cups

1/4 cup yellow mustard seeds
8 bay leaves
2 tablespoons black peppercorns
2 tablespoons crushed red pepper flakes
4 teaspoons celery seeds
1 tablespoon coriander seeds
1 tablespoon ground ginger
1 teaspoon ground mace
1/4 cup salt
2 tablespoons chili powder
2 tablespoons cayenne pepper

Using a spice mill, a mortar and pestle, or a coffee mill (see Note), process the mustard seeds, bay leaves, peppercorns, red pepper flakes, celery seeds, and coriander seeds until ground to a powder. Pour the mixture into a medium bowl and stir in the remaining ingredients. Store in an airtight container. The mixture is good until you use it up, so keep it dry and sealed.

Note: Make sure the coffee mill you use is dedicated to grinding only seeds, spices, and dried herbs.

Cream of Watercress Soup with Herbal Drop Scones

Noel Cullen/ Reprinted from *Elegant Irish Cooking* (Lebhar-Friedman Books)

Serves 8

*Leeks and potatoes is a classic combination that always make a
wonderful soup; adding watercress with its mild peppery flavor adds a great dimension,
as do the panfried drop scones.*

Soup
1 large onion, diced
½ cup diced leek
½ cup diced celery
2 tablespoons butter
2 potatoes, peeled and diced
1 quart chicken or vegetable stock
½ cup heavy cream
6 ounces watercress, well washed
½ cup whipped heavy cream, for garnish
8 sprigs watercress, for garnish

Drop Scones
¾ cup all-purpose flour
1 teaspoon salt
1 teaspoon baking powder
2 tablespoons milk
2 eggs
¼ cup (½ stick) melted butter
1 tablespoon chopped mixed fresh herbs, such
    as parsley, basil, and rosemary
4 tablespoons safflower oil

To make the soup, in a 2-quart heavy-bottomed saucepan over medium-high heat, sweat the onion, leek, and celery in butter until soft.

Add the potatoes and stock. Simmer gently, uncovered, 25 minutes.

Add the cream and watercress and simmer, 2 minutes. In a food processor fitted with a steel blade, purée until smooth. Season to taste.

To make the scones, sift together the flour, salt, and baking powder. Blend in the milk, eggs, butter, and herbs. Pass this batter through a fine-mesh sieve into a small bowl. Refrigerate, covered with plastic wrap, 10 minutes.

Heat the safflower oil in a heavy-bottomed pan. Pour a tablespoon of batter in the pan. Cook on both sides, about 30 to 40 seconds per side or until golden brown. Remove to a plate and keep warm. Repeat with the remaining batter.

Ladle the soup into soup plates and garnish each with a dollop of whipped cream and a sprig of watercress. Serve the scones alongside.

Pacific Northwest Salmon Chowder

Jasper White/Reprinted from *50 Chowders* (Scribner & Son)

Makes about 13 cups (serves 6 to 8 as a main course)

*Chowder is the ultimate one-pot meal and no one makes it more ultimate
than the king of New England cooking, Jasper White. In this chowder, he gives a nod
to the West Coast with the use of salmon.*

20 spring onions, 1 pint pearl onions, or
   12 ounces small boiling onions
4 ounces slab (unsliced) bacon, rind removed and
   cut into ⅓-inch dice
4 tablespoons unsalted butter
2 shallots (2 ounces), finely diced
2 dried bay leaves
2 to 3 sprigs fresh summer savory or thyme,
   leaves removed and chopped (1 teaspoon)
2 to 3 sprigs fresh tarragon, leaves removed and
   chopped (1 teaspoon)
2 pounds Yukon Gold, Main, PEI, or other all-purpose
   potatoes, peeled and sliced ⅓ inch thick
4 cups Traditional Fish Stock (page 46), chicken
   stock, or water (as a last resort)
Kosher or sea salt and freshly ground black pepper
3 pounds skinless salmon fillets, pinbones
   removed and cut into large chunks
1½ cups heavy cream (or up to 2 cups if desired)
2 tablespoons very coarsely chopped fresh chervil
   or chopped fresh flat-leaf parsley, for garnish

Remove all the tough outer leaves from the spring onions and trim them to about 1 inch long so they have only a little of the green top attached. Blanch the onions in a 2-quart saucepan of boiling salted water for 3 to 4 minutes. Using a slotted spoon, transfer them to a bowl of ice water to cool, then drain. Cut the larger ones lengthwise in half; reserve until later. If you are using pearl onions, blanch them in their skins for 3 minutes, then transfer to ice water; drain and peel. If you are using small boiling onions, blanch in their skins for 5 minutes, transfer to ice water, drain, and peel; trim them down in size if needed.

Heat a 4- to 6-quart heavy pot over low heat and add the diced bacon. Once it has rendered a few tablespoons of fat, increase the heat to medium and cook until the bacon is crisp and golden brown. Pour off all but 1 tablespoon of the bacon fat, leaving the bacon in the pot.

Add the butter, shallots, and bay leaves and sauté, stirring often with a wooden spoon, for 2 minutes. Stir in the savory or thyme and tarragon and cook 1 minute longer. Add the potatoes and stock. If the stock doesn't cover the potatoes, add just enough water to cover them. Turn up the heat and bring to a boil, cover, and cook the potatoes vigorously for about 10 minutes, until they are soft on the outside but still firm on the inside. If the stock hasn't thickened lightly, smash a few potato slices against the side of the pot and cook for 1 to 2 minutes longer to release their starch. Add the blanched onions, reduce the heat to low, and simmer for 5 minutes. Season the mixture assertively with salt and pepper (you want to almost overseason the chowder at this point, to avoid having to stir it much once the fish is added).

Add the salmon and cook for 5 minutes, then remove from the heat and allow the chowder to sit for 10 minutes. (The fish will finish cooking during this time.) Gently stir in the cream and adjust the seasoning if necessary. If you are not serving the chowder within the hour, let it cool a bit, then refrigerate; cover after it has completely chilled. Otherwise, let it sit for up to an hour at room temperature, allowing the flavors to meld.

When ready to serve, reheat the chowder over low heat; don't let it boil. Use a slotted spoon to place the chunks of salmon, the potatoes, and spring onions in the center of large soup plates or shallow bowls, and ladle the creamy broth around. Sprinkle with the chopped chervil.

Variation: Pacific Northwest Salmon Chowder with Peas

1 pound fresh peas, shucked (about 1 cup)
2 tablespoons unsalted butter
Kosher or sea salt and freshly ground black pepper

Blanch the shucked peas in boiling salted water for 1 minute. Drain them in a small colander or strainer and rinse them under cold water to stop the cooking.

Make the salmon chowder as directed, but reduce the butter by 2 tablespoons. Right before you dish up the chowder, warm the peas with the 2 tablespoons butter in a small sauté pan over low heat. Season the peas with the salt and pepper and spoon them, with the butter, over the individual servings of chowder.

Traditional Fish Stock
Makes about 2 quarts

4 pounds fish frames (bones) from sole, flounder,
   halibut, and/or turbot, cut into 2-inch pieces
   and rinsed clean of any blood
½ cup dry white wine
About 2 quarts water
2 onions, very thinly sliced
2 stalks celery, very thinly sliced
2 carrots, very thinly sliced
2 dried bay leaves
¼ cup roughly chopped fresh flat-leaf parsley
   leaves and stems
6 to 8 sprigs fresh thyme
2 tablespoons black peppercorns
Kosher or sea salt

In a 7- to 8-quart stockpot, combine the fish bones, white wine, and just enough water to cover (you won't need the full 2 quarts of water here). Bring to a boil, skimming off the white foam from the top of the stock as it approaches boiling, then reduce the heat so the stock simmers. (Using a ladle and a circular motion, push the foam from the center to the outside of the pot, where it is easy to remove.)

Add the onions, celery, carrots, bay leaves, parsley, thyme, and peppercorns and stir them into the liquid. If the ingredients are not covered by the liquid, add a little more water. Allow the stock to simmer gently for 20 minutes.

Remove the stock from the stove, stir it again, and allow it to steep for 10 minutes. Strain through a fine-mesh sieve and season lightly with salt. If you are not going to be using the stock within the hour, chill it as quickly as possible. Cover the stock after it has completely cooled and keep refrigerated for up to 3 days or freeze for up to 2 months.

Smoked Sablefish and Oyster Stew

Robert Clark, Executive Chef at Rain City Grill and C Restaurant

Serves 4

Sablefish works well in a variety of cooking styles due to its rich oil content and delicate white meat. It is exceptionally flavorful and an excellent fish for smoking.

6 ounces smoked sablefish
6 medium oysters, shucked
1 tablespoon butter
6 shallots, sliced into rings
½ cup finely diced carrots
2 cloves garlic
½ cup white wine
½ cup vermouth
1 cup 35% cream
4 baby potatoes, blanched and diced
½ cup spinach, blanched
1 lemon, cut in half

Place the sablefish in a small pot covered with water. Simmer gently until cooked. Remove the fish and allow to cool. Bring 1 cup of the poaching liquid back to a boil and add the shucked oysters, remove from the heat, let sit until needed.

In a saucepan, melt the butter and sweat the shallots, carrots, and garlic until tender. Remove the garlic and pour in the wine and vermouth. Reduce until thick. Pour in 1 cup of the poaching liquid and return to a boil. Reduce by half, add the cream, and return to a simmer. Chop up 2 of the oysters and add to the cream. Add the diced potatoes and remove from the heat.

Divide the spinach into 4 hot soup bowls. Place one oyster on each pile of spinach and pour over the hot soup. Drizzle with a touch of lemon.

Minestrone Genovese (Genoese Vegetable Soup)

Editors of *Saveur* Magazine/Reprinted from *Saveur Cooks Authentic Italian* (Chronicle Books)

Serves 4

This is the real thing, according to Saveur *editor Colman Andrews.*
Short noodles (tubetti pasta) give this minestrone its authentic Genoese look and taste,
as does a finishing touch of pesto.

1 ounce dried porcini mushrooms
¼ pound Swiss chard, stems removed
¼ pound spinach, stems removed
Salt
2 small zucchini, diced
2 white potatoes, peeled and diced
2 Japanese eggplants, peeled and diced
2 tablespoons extra virgin olive oil
2 cups tubetti pasta
2 cups cooked white beans
2 tablespoons pesto*
Freshly ground black pepper

Soak the mushrooms in 2 cups warm water until soft, about 20 minutes. Remove the mushrooms, rinse, chop, and set aside. Pour mushroom water through a coffee filter and reserve. Chop chard and spinach leaves.

Bring mushroom water and 6 cups salted water to a boil in a large pot. Add mushrooms, chard, spinach, zucchini, potatoes, eggplant, and olive oil. Reduce heat to low and simmer, uncovered, for 1 hour.

Add the pasta to the soup. Cook the pasta for about 10 minutes, add the beans, and cook 5 minutes longer. Stir in the pesto and season with salt and pepper. Serve hot or, in the Genoese tradition, at room temperature. Sprinkle with grated Parmigiano-Reggiano, if you like.

Note: You may substitute or add cauliflower, turnips, carrots, and/or other fresh vegetables to the ingredients called for—but don't use stock. The vegetables make their own.

*To make your own pesto, process 2 tightly packed cups stemless basil leaves, 2 tablespoons pine nuts, 2 cloves peeled and chopped garlic, coarse salt, ½ cup mild extra virgin olive oil, and ½ cup Parmigiano-Reggiano in a food processor.

Dungeness Crab and Celery Root Salad

Robert Clark, Executive Chef at Rain City Grill and C Restaurant

Serves 4

Even though celery root (or celeriac) is still more commonly used in Europe than in the United States, it is becoming more and more popular here as cooks discover how much it enhances salads, soups, and stews with its pungent, celery-like flavor.

1 cup julienned celery root
2 Granny Smith apples, julienned
2 tablespoons mayonnaise
2 tablespoons champagne vinegar
2 tablespoons Dijon mustard
½ cup crushed hazelnuts
Salt and pepper
½ cup flat-leaf parsley leaves
2 tablespoons hazelnut oil
8 ounces Dungeness crabmeat

Toss the celery root and apples in a bowl with the mayonnaise, vinegar, mustard, and hazelnuts. Season to taste with salt and pepper.

In a separate bowl, toss the parsley, hazelnut oil, and crabmeat.

Refrigerate for 20 minutes. Divide the celery root mixture among 4 plates, top with the crabmeat, and serve.

Creamy Tortellini Salad

Abigail Johnson Dodge/Reprinted from Williams-Sonoma's *The Kid's Cookbook* (Time-Life Books)

Serves 4

This is an excellent recipe for children or beginner cooks. The salad has a creamy yogurt and cream cheese dressing with fresh herbs for added flavor.

3 ounces cream cheese, at room temperature
½ cup plain yogurt
1 tablespoon finely chopped fresh dill
1 tablespoon finely chopped fresh chives
1 small clove garlic, finely chopped
Salt and pepper
3 quarts water
1 large carrot, peeled
9 ounces fresh cheese-filled tortellini (about 2 cups)
¼ pound green beans, ends trimmed and cut into 1-inch pieces
2 tablespoons milk

In a small mixing bowl, mix together with a wooden spoon the cream cheese, yogurt, dill, chives, and garlic until smooth. Season to taste with salt and pepper. Set the dressing aside.

Pour the water into a large pot and add 2 teaspoons salt. Cover, set the pot over high heat, and bring the water to a rolling boil.

Meanwhile, shred the carrot: Using the large holes of a box grater-shredder, rub the carrot over the holes in short strokes to form thin, short strips. Set the shredded carrot aside.

When the water is at a rolling boil, slowly and carefully add the tortellini. Be careful: The water and steam are very hot! Using a slotted spoon, stir the tortellini so that they don't stick together.

Reduce the heat to medium-high and boil gently for 4 minutes, stirring occasionally.

Add the cut-up beans to the pot with the tortellini and continue to boil for 2 more minutes. Add the shredded carrot to the pot and continue to cook until the pasta is al dente (tender but still firm to the bite) and the vegetables are tender, about 1 minute longer.

Set a colander in the sink. Have potholders ready. Ask an adult to help you pour the contents of the pot into the colander. Rinse the pasta and vegetables with cold water and drain well.

Dump the drained pasta and vegetables into a serving bowl. Add the dressing and the 2 tablespoons milk. Gently toss the salad with the wooden spoon until well blended. Season with salt and pepper. Serve warm or chilled.

Salad of Frisée and Tangerine with Grilled Sweet Potato

Fritz Sonnenschmidt, CMC, AAC/Reprinted from *American Harvest* (Lebhar-Friedman Books)

Serves 6

If you like sweet potatoes, you'll love them grilled. Use the variety with the dark orange flesh—which are sometimes mistakenly called "yams." The use of frisée, the French term for chicory or curly endive, makes a tasty and attractive addition to the salad.

2 sweet potatoes, well rinsed
¾ cup olive or peanut oil
¼ cup flat-leaf parsley leaves
3 tablespoons soy sauce
2 tablespoons orange juice
5 cloves garlic, crushed
¼ cup white wine, such as Riesling or chardonnay
2 tablespoons honey mustard
1 tablespoon balsamic vinegar
1 teaspoon poppyseeds, toasted (see Note)
4 tangerines, peeled, sectioned, membranes removed
1 tablespoon chopped fresh chervil, or
 ½ teaspoon dried
Salt and freshly ground black pepper
1 head frisée, cored, well rinsed, and spun dry

Preheat the oven to 350 degrees F.

Bake or boil the sweet potatoes until they are ¾ cooked, about 20 minutes; a sharp knife should enter the flesh with a little resistance. Let cool slightly, peel and discard the skin, and slice into ¼-inch thick rounds.

In a medium bowl, combine ¼ cup of the oil, the parsley, soy sauce, orange juice, and crushed garlic. Stir to combine, add the sweet potato slices, mixing and turning them to coat evenly. Set aside for at least 10 minutes or up to 1 hour.

Preheat the grill. When hot, brush the grill rack with oil. Add the sweet potato slices and cook on both sides until just cooked through.

To prepare the dressing, combine the remaining ½ cup oil, white wine, honey mustard, balsamic vinegar, and poppyseeds in a large bowl. Whisk to blend. Add the tangerine segments and chervil; season with salt and pepper. Fold in the frisée, evenly coating with dressing. Portion the salad onto serving plates. Top with the grilled sweet potato slices.

Note: To toast the poppyseeds, place the seeds in a skillet over medium-low heat and cook, stirring frequently to prevent burning, until fragrant and lightly toasted, about 2 minutes.

Roasted Asparagus and Orange Salad, Asparagus "Fettuccine"

Rozanne Gold/Reprinted from *Healthy 1 - 2 - 3* (Stewart Tabori & Chang)

Serves 4

This recipe has an ingenious trick in which asparagus is shaved into long strips with a peeler and ends up looking like fettuccine. The combination of oranges and asparagus is not only delicious, but makes a beautiful plate.

1³/₄ pounds thick asparagus
2 tablespoons olive oil
¹/₂ teaspoon kosher salt
Freshly ground black pepper
4 large oranges
Sea salt

Preheat the oven to 500 degrees F.

Snap off the woody bottoms of the asparagus and discard. Using a vegetable peeler, gently peel skin of asparagus in long thin strips. Set aside. Cut the peeled asparagus spears into 3 pieces on the bias. Place the cut asparagus in a bowl with ¹/₂ tablespoon olive oil, 1/2 teaspoon kosher salt, and freshly ground black pepper. Toss to coat thoroughly.

Transfer asparagus to a baking sheet, making one layer. Roast for 12 minutes, shaking several times to prevent sticking.

Meanwhile, grate the rind of 1 orange to yield ¹/₂ teaspoon zest. Cut 2 oranges in half and squeeze ¹/₂ cup juice. Place the juice, 1¹/₂ tablespoons olive oil, and zest in a blender. Blend until slightly emulsified. Add a pinch of sea salt and pepper to taste. Set aside.

Peel and segment the remaining oranges: Using a small sharp knife, cut off the 2 polar ends of each orange. Cut down the sides of the oranges to remove all peel and white pith. Gently cut down the side of each segment, right next to the membrane, and out again at the next membrane, releasing the segment but leaving the membrane behind. Set aside.

Transfer the asparagus with any oil to a bowl. Cover to keep warm.

Bring a pot of salted water to a boil. Add the reserved asparagus peelings ("fettuccine") and cook for 5 to 6 minutes until bright and tender. Drain in a colander and refresh in a bowl of cold water. Pat dry.

Carefully toss the asparagus with the orange segments. Add salt and pepper to taste. Mound the asparagus in the center of 4 large plates. Top with asparagus "fettuccine." Pour the dressing over the salad. Serve warm or at room temperature.

Warm Goat Cheese and Beet Salad

Michael Lomonaco

Serves 4 to 6

Warm goat cheese is a treat that never goes out of style and when served with miniature yellow and red beets, it's especially memorable. This recipe comes from one of New York's most renowned and talented chefs, Michael Lomonaco.

1 (10-ounce) log fresh goat cheese
¼ cup flour
2 eggs, beaten with 2 tablespoons water
½ cup dry bread crumbs
2 bunches (about 1 pound) miniature or young yellow and red beets
1 quart water
1 tablespoon plus ½ teaspoon salt
3 tablespoons plus ¼ cup olive oil
1 cup mixed mesclun greens or other assorted lettuce leaves
2 tablespoons lemon juice
Freshly ground black pepper to taste
1 tablespoon balsamic vinegar, preferably an aged vinegar

Cut the goat cheese log into 8 equal pieces. Dip the cheese into the flour, before dipping into the beaten egg and then finally into the bread crumbs to create an even coating. Set aside.

Clean the beets of most of their green tops, leaving only the last 1 or 2 inches of greens. In a soup pot, bring the water and 1 tablespoon of the salt to a boil. Place the golden beets into the boiling water and cook until the beets are tender, about 3 to 4 minutes, before removing and refreshing in ice water. Repeat the process with the red beets, keeping them separate to keep the red beets from staining the golden beets. After they have cooled completely, slip the beets out of their skins by using paper towels to grasp the beets at the same time as you pull off the outside skins. Cut the beets into halves if they are especially large and set aside.

Heat 3 tablespoons of the olive oil in a small skillet, add the bread crumb-coated goat cheese and sauté until golden brown, about 1 or 2 minutes, before turning to brown the second side. Cook all the cheese rounds in this fashion.

Combine the beets with the mesclun salad, adding the remaining ¼ cup olive oil and the lemon juice. Season with the remaining ½ teaspoon salt and freshly ground black pepper, and toss to coat well. Place equal portions of the salad onto plates and top each off with a disk or two of warm goat cheese. Drizzle some balsamic vinegar over the top and serve.

Challah

Lauren Groveman/Reprinted from *Lauren Groveman's Kitchen* (Chronicle Books)

Makes 2 large braided freestanding loaves

Challah, a sweet egg bread usually braided, is a symbolic bread in the Jewish religion served on their Sabbath. There are many different versions, but this one from Home Cooking *host Lauren Groveman is particularly delicious and foolproof.*

3 tablespoons plus ½ cup (1 stick) unsalted
　butter, at room temperature
1 cup milk
⅓ cup sugar, plus a pinch of sugar for yeast
1 tablespoon mild-flavored honey
2½ teaspoons salt
2 packages active dry yeast
½ cup lukewarm water
4 extra large eggs, made tepid by steeping whole
　egg (in shell) in hot tap water for 10 minutes
Up to 6 cups high-gluten (high-protein) bread
　flour, including flour for dusting
Cornmeal, preferably medium-ground, for baking
　sheet
1 egg beaten with 1 egg yolk and 1 tablespoon
　cream or water, for glaze

Optional Toppings
Sesame, poppy, and/or whole caraway seeds
Reconstituted toasted dried onions or fresh
　onions, minced and sautéed in vegetable oil
　until translucent and cooled
Kosher sea salt

Melt 3 tablespoons butter and brush the interior of an 8-quart mixing bowl with the butter. Set bowl aside for rising dough.

Cut the remaining ½ cup butter into small pieces and place in a small saucepan with milk. Heat milk over low heat until just warm throughout and pour into a large mixing bowl. Stir in ⅓ cup sugar, honey, and salt. Dissolve yeast in the luke-warm water with a pinch of sugar. When creamy and starting to bubble, add to mixing bowl along with the eggs. Stir well with a wooden spoon.

Stir in just enough flour, a little at a time, to create a mass that leaves the sides of the bowl and is not easily stirred. Knead dough in a brisk push, fold, and turning motion, until perfectly smooth and elastic, adding only as much flour as necessary to keep the dough from sticking to your hands and work surface.

When the dough is of the proper consistency, place it in the buttered rising bowl and brush the top with more melted butter. Cover the bowl with buttered plastic wrap and a clean kitchen towel and let rise in a warm, draft-free spot until double in bulk, about 2 hours. Uncover the bowl and punch down the dough with several swift swats with the back of your hand, totally deflating the dough. Re-cover the bowl and let it rise until doubled, about 1 hour and 15 minutes.

Line 2 large shallow baking sheets with parchment paper and sprinkle the paper with cornmeal. On a lightly floured work surface, use the blade of your pastry scraper to divide the dough in half. Cover one half as you work with the other. Divide 1 section of dough into 3 equal pieces. Roll each piece into a strand about 10 inches long with tapered ends and slightly chubby centers. (Use extra flour only as necessary to keep dough from sticking to your hands and work surface; too much flour will prevent traction necessary for rolling strands.)

Align the strands and beginning in the center (going down) braid as you would braid hair, alternately bringing outside strands over the center strand. Turn the braided portion up so the unbraided strands point down and continue to braid—but this time bring the center strand alternately over the outside left strand and then the right strand until you reach the bottom. Pinch to seal and tuck all pinched ends underneath. Repeat dividing, rolling, and braiding procedure with the other section of dough. Place each loaf on the prepared baking sheet, gently "plump" the loaves, and realign the shapes. Cover with a kitchen towel and let rise 40 minutes. (If not working with a double oven, you can bake both loaves at the same time in the upper and lower third shelves of the oven by switching positions after half the baking time; or allow 1 braided loaf to rise in the refrigerator until the first loaf enters the oven.)

Preheat the oven to 375 degrees F.

To glaze the loaves, push the egg glaze through a medium-mesh strainer into a small bowl. Using a pastry brush, paint the exposed surface of the loaves gently and thoroughly with the glaze. Let the glaze set for 5 minutes and reapply. (Reserve any remaining glaze to use if necessary during baking.) If desired, sprinkle tops and sides of loaves generously with sesame, poppy, and/or caraway seeds. Even if you don't add seeds, I suggest that you lightly sprinkle the tops with coarse salt.

Bake the loaves until they are golden, feel light when lifted, and sound hollow when tapped on the bottom, 35 to 45 minutes. (If applicable, remove chilled braid from the refrigerator as soon as the first loaf enters the oven to continue rising at room temperature.) Check the braided loaves after baking 20 minutes; as the dough expands in the oven, new dough will become exposed. Brush these white spots with a little of the reserved glaze and continue to bake. Cover the top loosely with aluminum foil (shiny side up) if the loaves become overly brown.

Remove the loaves from the oven and cool thoroughly on a rack to allow the interior to relax and expand before slicing and reheating. (If applicable, glaze, top, and bake the remaining braided loaf as directed.)

Sandwich Loaf

Lauren Groveman/Reprinted from *Lauren Groveman's Kitchen* (Chronicle Books)

Makes three 8 by 4-inch loaves

Lauren Groveman's Challah is a particularly versatile recipe that can be made into many different shapes and sizes. You'll find it works exceptionally well as a sandwich loaf.

1 recipe Challah dough (page 56)

Prepare Challah dough as directed through 2 risings. Generously grease 3 (8 by 4-inch) loaf pans with melted butter and sprinkle the interiors lightly with cornmeal. Shake out the excess. Uncover fully risen dough and punch down once more. Turn dough out onto a lightly floured board and, using the blade of your pastry scraper, divide the dough into 3 equal sections. Keep the dough covered as you work with 1 piece at a time.

Lay 1 section of dough on a lightly floured board and flatten gently with your hand. Using gentle, deliberate, and even pressure with a rolling pin, roll out the dough into an 8 by 10-inch rectangle. (To ensure an even thickness, don't roll over the ends but just up to them. If the dough loses its shape while rolling, simply knock the sides back in place with the long side of the pin.) Starting with the short end of the rectangle, roll the dough jelly-roll style into a snug log, pinching after each revolution to remove any air pockets. When you get to the bottom of the rectangle, pull up the last lip of dough and pinch well to seal. Lift up 1 end of the log to expose the coil created by rolling. With your fingers, gently push in the coil toward the center. Pinch the outer rim of dough together, pulling to elongate it slightly. Pull down the elongated section to attach to the seam. Repeat on the other end of the rolled dough. Rotate the loaf gently back and forth on your floured board to plump the shape and lay the loaf, seam side down, in a buttered loaf pan. Repeat rolling and shaping the other 2 loaves. Cover and let rise 45 minutes.

Preheat the oven to 375 degrees F if using metal pans and 350 degrees F if using glass.

Glaze, top, and bake the loaves until they are golden, feel light when lifted, and sound hollow when tapped on the bottom, 30 to 35 minutes.

Remove the loaves from the oven and cool thoroughly on a rack to allow the interior to relax and expand before slicing and reheating.

Note: Alternately, the dough may be shaped into braids as directed in the Challah recipe and baked in the prepared loaf pans, plump side down.

Raisin Loaves with Cinnamon Swirl

Lauren Groveman/Reprinted from *Lauren Groveman's Kitchen* (Chronicle Books)

Makes three 8 by 4-inch loaves

Here's another way to use the Challah dough for a sweet raisin bread
from Home Cooking's *host, Lauren Groveman.*

3 tablespoons plus ½ cup (1 stick) unsalted
   butter, at room temperature
1 cup milk
2 cups raisins (mix light and dark)
⅓ cup sugar, plus a pinch of sugar for yeast
1 tablespoon mild-flavored honey
2½ teaspoons salt
2 packages active dry yeast
½ cup lukewarm water
4 extra large eggs, made tepid by steeping whole
   egg (in shell) in hot tap water for 10 minutes
Up to 6 cups high-gluten (high-protein) bread
   flour, including flour for dusting

Cinnamon Sugar
2 tablespoons ground cinnamon
1 cup granulated sugar

Melt 3 tablespoons butter and brush the interior of an 8-quart mixing bowl with the butter. Set bowl aside for rising dough.

Cut the remaining ½ cup butter into small pieces and place in a small saucepan with milk. Scald the milk over medium heat and pour into a large mixing bowl. Stir in the raisins, ⅓ cup sugar, honey, and salt. Allow the raisins to plump as the milk becomes lukewarm. Dissolve yeast in the lukewarm water with a pinch of sugar. When creamy and starting to bubble, add to mixing bowl along with the eggs. Stir well with a wooden spoon.

Stir in just enough flour, a little at a time, to create a mass that leaves the sides of the bowl and is not easily stirred. Knead dough in a brisk push, fold, and turning motion, until perfectly smooth and elastic, adding only as much flour as necessary to keep the dough from sticking to your hands and work surface.

When the dough is of the proper consistency, place it in the buttered rising bowl and brush the top with more melted butter. Cover the bowl with buttered plastic wrap and a clean kitchen towel and let rise in a warm, draft-free spot until double in bulk, about 2½ hours. Uncover the bowl and punch down the dough with several swift swats with the back of your hand, totally deflating the dough. Re-cover the bowl and let it rise until doubled, about 1½ hours.

Meanwhile make the Cinnamon Sugar. Whisk the cinnamon with the sugar in a small bowl. If the sugar is lumpy, sift the mixture through a triple-mesh wire sieve after whisking. (Store in a large screw-top jar at comfortable room temperature away from direct sunlight.)

Generously grease 3 (8 by 4-inch) loaf pans with melted butter. Uncover fully risen dough and punch down once more. Turn dough out onto a lightly floured board and, using the blade of your pastry scraper, divide the dough into 3 equal sections. Keep the dough covered as you work with 1 piece at a time.

Lay 1 section of dough on a lightly floured board and flatten gently with your hand. Using gentle, deliberate, and even pressure with a rolling pin, roll out the dough into an 8 by 10-inch rectangle. (To ensure an even thickness, don't roll over the ends but just up to them. If the dough loses its shape while rolling, simply knock the sides back in place with the long side of the pin.) Sprinkle ¼ cup Cinnamon Sugar, spreading it out to cover the entire surface of the rectangle. Starting with the short end of the rectangle, roll the dough jelly-roll style into a tight log. When you get to the bottom of the rectangle, pull up the last lip of dough and pinch well to seal. Lift up 1 end of the log to expose the coil created by rolling. With your fingers, gently push in the coil toward the center. (But be careful: If you push in too far, you

will lose some of the spiral design created by the cinnamon sugar.) Pinch the outer rim of dough together, pulling to elongate it slightly. Pull down the elongated section to attach to the seam. Repeat on the other end of the rolled dough. Rotate the loaf gently back and forth on your floured board to plump the shape and lay the loaf, seam side down, in a buttered loaf pan. Repeat rolling and shaping the other 2 loaves. Cover and let rise 45 minutes.

Preheat the oven to 375 degrees F if using metal pans and 350 degrees F if using glass.

Bake the loaves until they are golden, feel light when lifted, and sound hollow when tapped on the bottom, 30 to 35 minutes.

Remove the loaves from the oven and cool thoroughly on a rack to allow the interior to relax and expand before slicing and reheating.

Chapter 4

MAINDISHES

Moroccan-Spiced Shrimp on Fruited Couscous

Rick Rodgers/Reprinted from *Simply Shrimp* (Chronicle Books)

Serves 4 to 6

Many people do not realize how simple it is to make couscous, which merely needs to sit in boiling water for about 5 to 7 minutes. It comes from North Africa, and to most people's surprise, it's not a grain, but pasta made from semolina.

Fruited Couscous
1 cup freshly squeezed orange juice
1 cup water
½ cup raisins
½ teaspoon salt
1 (10-ounce) box quick-cooking couscous (1½ cups)

2 tablespoons extra virgin olive oil
1 onion, chopped
2 carrots, cut into ¼-inch-thick rounds
2 zucchini, cut into ¼-inch cubes
2 cloves garlic, minced
1 teaspoon sweet Hungarian paprika
1 teaspoon ground cumin
½ teaspoon ground coriander
¼ teaspoon cayenne
¼ teaspoon salt
⅛ teaspoon crushed saffron threads
1 (-ounce) can plum tomatoes, drained and chopped
2 tablespoons freshly squeezed lemon juice
1 teaspoon sugar
1 cup Shrimp Stock (page 75) or chicken broth
1 pound medium shrimp, peeled and deveined

In a medium saucepan, bring the orange juice, water, raisins, and salt to a boil over high heat. Stir in the couscous. Remove from the heat and cover tightly. Let stand for 5 minutes or until the couscous absorbs the liquid.

In a large (12-inch) nonstick skillet, heat the oil over medium-high heat. Add the onions and carrots. Stir until the onion is golden, about 5 minutes. Add the zucchini and cook until almost tender, about 4 minutes. Add the garlic, paprika, cumin, coriander, cayenne, salt, and saffron and stir for 30 seconds. Add the tomatoes, lemon juice, and sugar and stir 1 minute. Add the stock and bring to a simmer. Cook until slightly reduced, about 2 minutes.

Add the shrimp and cover the skillet. Cook until the shrimps are pink and firm, 2 to 3 minutes. Serve immediately, spooned over the couscous.

Chicken Breasts in Jambalaya Sauce

Rick Rodgers/Reprinted from *On Rice* (Chronicle Books)

Serves 4 to 6

Like most traditional jambalaya found in Louisiana, this dish combines meat, poultry, and shrimp along with tomatoes, green pepper, and onion to create a flavorful and rich stew. Try to use a high-quality sausage for the best results.

1 tablespoon vegetable oil, or more as needed
3 (9-ounce) chicken breast halves with skin and bones, chopped in half vertically to make 6 pieces
¼ teaspoon salt
¼ teaspoon freshly ground black pepper
6 ounces smoked sausage, such as andouille, chorizo, or kielbasa, cut into ½-inch pieces
1 onion, chopped
1 bell pepper, seeded and chopped
1 stalk celery with leaves, chopped
1 clove garlic, minced
1½ teaspoons Cajun seasoning
1 cup canned crushed tomatoes
1 cup homemade chicken broth or low-sodium canned broth
8 ounces medium shrimp, peeled and deveined
Steamed rice, preferably long-grain rice

In a large Dutch oven or flameproof casserole, heat the oil over medium-high heat. In batches, add the chicken breast pieces, skin side down, and cook, turning once until lightly browned, about 5 minutes. Transfer to a plate, leaving the fat in the pan. Season the breasts with salt and pepper and set aside.

Add more oil to the Dutch oven if needed. Add the sausage and reduce the heat to medium. Cook, stirring often, until the sausage is lightly browned, about 5 minutes. Add the onion, bell pepper, celery, and garlic. Cook, stirring often, until the vegetables soften, about 5 minutes.

Stir in the Cajun seasoning and cook 1 minute.

Stir in the crushed tomatoes and chicken broth and bring to a simmer. Return the chicken breasts to the Dutch oven and reduce heat to medium-low. Simmer until the chicken shows no sign of pink when pierced in the thickest part, 15 to 20 minutes. Transfer the chicken to a plate and cover with aluminum foil to keep warm.

Skim any fat from the surface of the sauce. Stir in the shrimp and cook just until they are pink and firm, about 3 minutes.

Spoon the rice onto individual dinner plates. Top each serving with the sauce and then a chicken breast. Serve immediately.

Coconut Shrimp with Easy Peanut Sauce

Rick Rodgers/Reprinted from *Simply Shrimp* (Chronicle)

Serves 6 to 8

Dipped in a beer batter, rolled with coconut, and deep-fried till golden brown, this is one of those hors d'oeuvres that will disappear quickly at any gathering. Author Rick Rodgers first ate them at the Fairmont Hotel in San Francisco and has artfully re-created a wonderful recipe.

Easy Peanut Sauce
⅓ cup chicken broth, preferably homemade, or low-sodium canned broth
¼ cup unsalted peanut butter
¼ cup hoisin sauce
1 tablespoon Asian fish sauce

Coconut Batter
1 cup all-purpose flour
1 teaspoon baking powder
1½ teaspoons Madras-style curry powder
½ teaspoon salt
⅛ teaspoon cayenne
1¼ cups flat lager beer
2 large eggs, beaten
1 cup unsweetened desiccated coconut (available at natural food stores)

Vegetable shortening, for deep-frying
1 pound extra-large to large shrimp, peeled with the tail segment left on and deveined

To make the sauce, whisk all of the ingredients in a small bowl and set aside. (The sauce can be prepared up to 2 hours ahead, covered, and kept at room temperature. If the sauce thickens upon standing, thin to a thick dipping consistency with broth or water.)

To make the batter, in a medium bowl, whisk the flour, baking powder, curry powder, salt, and cayenne to mix. Add the beer and eggs and stir with a spoon just until combined (do not overmix). Fold in ½ cup of the coconut. Place the remaining coconut on a plate.

Preheat the oven to 200 degrees F. Place a wire cake rack over a jelly-roll pan.

In a large, heavy saucepan, melt enough vegetable shortening over medium-high heat to come 3 inches up the sides of the pan and heat to 360 degrees F. Working in batches, dip the shrimps, one at a time, in the batter, then roll them in the coconut. Deep-fry until golden, 2 to 3 minutes. Using a slotted skimmer, transfer the shrimps to the wire rack and keep warm in the oven. Repeat with the remaining shrimps, batter, and coconut, allowing the shortening to return to 360 degrees F before frying each batch. Serve immediately, with the peanut sauce for dipping.

Pine Needle–Smoked Mussels

Ted Reader and Kathleen Sloan/Reprinted from *The Sticks and Stones Cookbook* (Macmillan Canada)

Serves 4 to 6

Using pine needles as a flavoring agent, Ted Reader, one of the most inventive grillers around, has come up with an ingenious way to grill mussels. Be sure to grill this in an open, well-ventilated space—not an apartment balcony or forest.

Kitchen bucket of pine needles
3 pounds fresh mussels, cleaned and debearded
3 tablespoons coarse sea salt
1 bunch fresh rosemary, leaves removed
    from stems
Juice of 2 limes
Freshly ground black pepper

Preheat grill to high.

Season mussels with sea salt. In a large mixing bowl, combine 3 or 4 handfuls of pine needles with rosemary. Mix well.

Place mussels directly on the grill, cover with pine needle-rosemary mixture, close lid, and let mussels grill-roast for 4 to 5 minutes until they open. Be careful when opening the lid; there will be a lot of smoke and ash. Blow or fan off the remaining ash and discard any unopened mussels. Place the mussels on a large serving platter, squeeze limes over them, season with black pepper and serve immediately with lots of warm crusty bread.

Korean Beef on Fiery Chinese Cabbage

Rick Rodgers/Reprinted from *On Rice* (Chronicle Books)

Serves 4 to 6

Like the one used here, Korean marinades typically have a thick, nearly paste-like mixture of soy sauce and sesame. While it's also typical to serve grilled or broiled meats with kimchi *(pickled cabbage), author Rick Rodgers uses a delicious, spicy Chinese cabbage stir-fry instead.*

Korean Marinade

1 tablespoon sesame seeds
1/3 cup soy sauce
2 scallions, finely chopped
1 tablespoon sugar
1 tablespoon Asian dark sesame oil
1 tablespoon minced ginger
1/4 teaspoon crushed red pepper flakes

1 1/2 pounds sirloin steak, trimmed, about
   3/4 inch thick

Spicy Chinese Cabbage

1 (1 1/2-pound) Chinese (napa) cabbage
1 tablespoon vegetable oil
3 scallions, chopped
1 tablespoon minced ginger
3 cloves garlic, minced
1/2 cup homemade chicken broth or low-sodium
   canned broth
1/2 teaspoon salt
1/4 teaspoon ground hot pepper
2 carrots, shredded
2 tablespoons rice vinegar

Steamed rice, preferably long-grain rice

To make the marinade, heat a medium-sized skillet over medium heat. Add the sesame seeds and cook, stirring almost constantly, until toasted and golden brown, about 3 minutes. Transfer to a plate to cool. In a mortar, or on a work surface with a heavy skillet, coarsely crush the sesame seeds. Place in a large shallow dish.

Add the remaining marinade ingredients and stir well to combine. Add the steak and rub some of the marinade ingredients over the top. Cover with plastic wrap and refrigerate for as long as possible, at least 1 hour or up to 8 hours.

To make the spicy cabbage, core and cut the cabbage crosswise into 1/2-inch strips. Heat a large (12-inch) nonstick skillet or wok over medium-high heat until hot. Add the oil, tilt the skillet to coat the bottom, and heat until the oil is very hot. Add the scallions, ginger, and garlic and stir-fry until very fragrant, about 30 seconds. Add the cabbage, chicken broth, salt, and hot pepper, Cook, uncovered, stirring often, until the cabbage strips are translucent and crisp-tender, about 5 minutes. Stir in the carrots and vinegar. Remove from the heat, cover, and keep warm.

Position a broiler rack 6 inches from the heat source and preheat the broiler. Remove the meat from the marinade, reserving the marinade.

Broil the meat, turning once, until cooked to desired doneness, about 7 minutes for medium-rare.

Meanwhile, pour the marinade into a small saucepan and bring to a boil over low heat. Simmer for 2 minutes. Set aside.

If necessary, reheat the cabbage. Cut the meat diagonally across the grain into ½-inch-thick slices. Spoon the rice into soup bowls. Top with the cabbage and then the sliced meat. Pour some of the marinade over each serving of meat, and serve immediately.

Scallops and Bacon Skewers with Maple-Lemon Glaze

Jasper White/From the menu at Summer Shack restaurant, Cambridge, Massachusetts

Serves 4

Jasper White's Summer Shack restaurant in Cambridge, Massachusetts, has been a phenomenon since its opening in 2000. Its seafood is unbeatable and the prices are shockingly low. If you can't make it there, try this recipe and you'll understand what the fuss is all about.

**20 jumbo (10/20 size) dry sea scallops
    (approximately 20 ounces)
5 ounces unsliced slab smoked bacon
Vegetable oil for grilling
Kosher salt and freshly ground black pepper
Maple-Lemon Glaze (recipe follows)**

Soak 10-inch bamboo skewers in water for a few hours to prevent them from burning on the grill. Preheat the oven to 325 degrees F. Prepare a gas or wood-fired grill to medium heat.

Pick through the scallops and remove the piece of attached "strap" from the side of the scallops. Keep the scallops refrigerated.

Trim the rind from the bacon and slice the slabs ⅓ inch thick. Cut the slices into 1-inch squares. Place them on a baking sheet and bake for about 12 minutes, until the bacon fat is rendered and the bacon is almost fully cooked. Drain the pieces on a paper towel.

To assemble the skewers, place a scallop flat side down on a board and push a skewer through the center, alternating the scallops with the rendered bacon. Each skewer should have 5 scallops and 4 pieces of bacon. (This can be made well ahead and refrigerated.)

Lightly oil the grill. Brush the skewers with oil and season lightly with salt and pepper. Place the scallops directly over the flame and cook for 1 minute. Turn the skewers over and brush with the Maple-Lemon Glaze. Cook 2 minutes more, then turn and glaze again. (The total cooking time is 5 to 6 minutes.) You can glaze the scallops one more time while they are on the grill. After you remove the scallops from the grill, you should glaze them one last time.

Maple-Lemon Glaze
Makes about ¾ cup

**1 cup maple syrup
¼ cup freshly squeezed lemon juice
Pinch of salt (or ¼ teaspoon)
Pinch of freshly ground black pepper
    (or ¼ teaspoon)**

Combine the maple syrup and lemon juice in a small saucepan and bring to a simmer over medium heat. Don't allow the mixture to boil, or it will foam and spill over.

Simmer the mixture for about 15 minutes until it has reduced to ¾ cup liquid. Season with salt and pepper and let cool to room temperature. There is no need to refrigerate this mixture. It handles best at room temperature. After it cools, cover it until ready to use.

Buttermilk Biscuits with Low Country Shrimp and Ham

Rick Rodgers/Reprinted from *Simply Shrimp* (Chronicle Books)

Serves 6

This is a wonderful dish for a sit-down brunch. In the South,
you might find it served with creamy grits instead of biscuits.

Buttermilk Biscuits

1 cup cake flour

1 cup bleached all-purpose flour

2 teaspoons cream of tartar

1 teaspoon baking soda

½ teaspoon salt

½ cup (1 stick) unsalted butter, chilled and cut into ½-inch cubes

¾ cup plus 2 tablespoons buttermilk

1 tablespoon unsalted butter

3 ounces (¼-inch-thick) Smithfield ham, Black Forest ham, or prosciutto, cut into ¼-inch-wide slivers

1½ pounds medium shrimp, peeled (reserve the shells for the stock) and deveined

½ cup chopped scallions, white and green parts

3 cups Shrimp Stock (recipe follows)

½ cup dry vermouth or additional broth

2 cups heavy cream

2 teaspoons chopped fresh tarragon or 1 teaspoon dried tarragon

¼ teaspoon salt

Hot red pepper sauce to taste

Preheat the oven to 400 degrees F.

To make the biscuits, sift the cake flour, all-purpose flour, cream of tartar, baking soda, and salt into a medium bowl. Using a pastry blender or 2 forks, cut in the butter until the mixture resembles coarse meal. Stirring with a fork, gradually pour as much buttermilk as needed to make a soft dough. Knead the dough lightly in the bowl just until it comes together. Do not over-work the dough. Turn out onto a lightly floured work surface. Roll into a ½-inch-thick circle. Using a 3-inch round biscuit cutter, cut out biscuits and place them on an ungreased baking sheet.

Gather the scraps and quickly and gently knead them back into a flat disk. Roll and cut out more biscuits and place on the baking sheet. (You will have 7 biscuits, which is 1 more than needed; the extra one is the cook's treat.) Bake until the biscuits are golden brown, 18 to 20 minutes. Remove from the oven, wrap in a clean kitchen towel to keep warm. (The biscuits can be prepared up to 2 hours ahead, cooled to room temperature, and reheated. Wrap the biscuits loosely in foil and bake in a preheated 350 degree F oven for 10 to 15 minutes, or until heated through.)

In a large nonstick skillet, heat the butter over medium-high heat. Add the ham and cook until it begins to brown, about 1 minute. Add the shrimp and scallions and cook, stirring occasionally, until the shrimp turn pink and firm, 2 to 3 minutes. Using a slotted spoon, transfer the shrimp and scallions to a bowl and set aside.

Add the stock and vermouth and bring to a boil over high heat. Boil until reduced by half, about 8 minutes. Add the cream, tarragon, and any accumulated juices from the bowl of shrimp. Boil until the sauce reduces enough to lightly coat a wooden spoon, about 5 minutes. Return the shrimp and scallions to the skillet, just to reheat, about 1 minute. Season with the salt and hot pepper sauce.

To serve, slice the biscuits in half horizontally. On each plate, place a biscuit, cut sides up. Spoon equal amounts of the creamed shrimp evenly over the biscuits. Serve immediately.

Shrimp Stock
Makes about 4 cups

Shells (and heads, if available) from 1 to 2 pounds of shrimp
1 cup bottled clam juice, canned low-sodium chicken broth, or additional water
1 small onion, chopped
1 small stalk celery with leaves
2 sprigs fresh parsley
⅛ teaspoon dried thyme
4 whole peppercorns
¼ teaspoon salt

In a medium saucepan, combine shrimp shells, 4 cups water, clam juice, onion, and celery. Bring to a boil over high heat, skimming off any foam that rises to the surface. Add the parsley, thyme, and peppercorns. Reduce heat to low and simmer for at least 15 and up to 30 minutes. Season with salt.

Strain the stock through a wire sieve, pressing hard on the shells to extract all of the stock. (The stock can be prepared up to 1 day ahead, cooled completely, covered, and refrigerated; it can be frozen for up to 1 month.)

Pork Loin Braised in Milk (Arrosto di Maiale nel Latte)

Biba Caggiano/Reprinted from *Biba's Taste of Italy* (HarperCollins Publishers)

Serves 6

Biba Caggiano showed us this wonderful recipe from the Emilia-Romagna region of Italy. Braising pork in milk results in a delicate taste and a rich, golden color from the cooked-down clusters of browned milk particles.

1 tablespoon chopped fresh rosemary or
  1 ½ teaspoons chopped dried rosemary
1 tablespoon finely chopped fresh sage or 3 to 4
  dried sage leaves, chopped
1 clove garlic, finely minced
Salt and freshly ground pepper to taste
1 (3- to 3 ½-pound) center-cut boneless pork
  loin roast
2 tablespoons unsalted butter
2 tablespoons extra virgin olive oil
3 to 4 cups whole milk

Combine the rosemary, sage, garlic, salt, and pepper in a small bowl and rub it all over the pork. Place the pork on a large plate, cover with plastic wrap, and refrigerate for a few hours.

Place a medium heavy pan that will hold the roast somewhat snugly over medium heat and add the butter and oil. When the butter begins to foam, add the pork and cook, turning occasionally, until lightly golden on all sides, 10 to 12 minutes. (Keep your eyes on the butter so it doesn't burn and reduce the heat a bit if needed.)

Add 1 cup of the milk and stir to loosen the browned bits attached to the bottom of the pan. As soon as the milk comes to a boil, reduce the heat to low, partially cover the pan, and simmer until almost all the milk has evaporated, about 15 minutes. Add 1 more cup of milk and continue cooking, basting and turning the meat a few

times, until most of the milk has evaporated. Cook the pork in this manner, adding the milk ½ to 1 cup at a time, until it reads 160 degrees F on an instant-read thermometer, about 2 hours. (The pork can be cooked up to this point 1 hour or so ahead. In that case, cook only until it reaches 155 degrees F, because it will keep on cooking as it sits in the pan juices.)

Remove the lid and raise the heat to high. If no more milk is left in the pan, add ½ cup or so more. Cook, stirring and scraping the bottom of the pan to release the browned bits and turning the pork once or twice, until most of the milk has evaporated and the meat has a rich, golden brown color. Transfer the pork to a cutting board and let it rest for about 10 minutes while you finish the sauce.

Spoon some of the fat from the pan. Add water, and stir quickly, over high heat, scraping the bottom of the pan until only brown glazed clusters of milk particles remain.

Cut the meat into ½-inch-thick slices and serve topped with a bit of the pan juices.

Jersey Shore Grilled Chicken, Tomato, and Crab

Thomas Bigan, CEC, AAC/Reprinted from *American Harvest* (Lebhar-Friedman Books)

Serves 6

This recipe comes from a book put together by the American Academy of Chefs, representing the work of some of the best chefs in America. It makes a beautiful presentation for a special occasion. If you can't find Jersey tomatoes, use any large, vine-ripened tomato.

½ cup olive oil
1 tablespoon chopped fresh parsley
1 teaspoon chopped fresh sage
½ teaspoon Old Bay Seasoning
Salt and freshly ground black pepper
6 boneless, skinless chicken breasts (about 5 ounces each)
3 Jersey tomatoes
2 tablespoons butter
1 teaspoon minced shallots
2 tablespoons dry white wine
2 cups half-and-half or light cream
1 ounce Gorgonzola cheese, crumbled
¼ cup freshly grated Parmesan cheese
2 ounces provolone cheese, diced
2 ounces fontina cheese, diced
½ cup seasoned bread crumbs
12 ounces jumbo lump crabmeat, picked clean
6 basil leaves, cut into long ribbons

In a small bowl, whisk the olive oil, parsley, sage, and Old Bay Seasoning, and season with salt and pepper.

Place the chicken breasts into a large shallow bowl or baking dish and pour the marinade over top, turning the chicken pieces to evenly coat, Cover and refrigerate at least 30 minutes.

Preheat the grill. Preheat the oven to 250 degrees F.

Cut the center core from the tomatoes and slice 4 thick slices from the center, leaving the 2 rounded ends, which should be diced. Set aside.

Heat 1 tablespoon of the butter in a medium saucepan over medium heat. Add the shallots and cook, stirring, 2 minutes. Add the diced tomatoes and cook another minute, then stir in the white wine. When the white wine is almost completely reduced, stir in the half-and-half and the cheeses. Heat just to a boil, reduce the heat, and simmer slowly, stirring constantly, until the sauce is creamy and thick enough to coat the back of a spoon, 2 to 3 minutes. Strain the sauce, then set aside and keep warm.

Spread the bread crumbs on a plate. Press the tomato slices into the crumbs, coating each side. Place the tomato slices onto the hot grill and cook until lightly browned, about 2 minutes per side.

Transfer to a plate and loosely cover to keep warm. Remove the chicken breasts from the marinade, wiping off any excess. Place them on the grill and cook, turning after 4 to 5 minutes, until cooked through, 10 to 12 minutes total. Transfer the cooked chicken to a platter and place in the oven to keep warm.

In a medium skillet, heat the remaining butter over medium-high heat. Add the crabmeat and cook, stirring, for about 5 minutes; season with salt and pepper.

To serve, place a chicken breast on each serving plate and top with a tomato slice, a spoonful of the crabmeat and the cheese sauce. Garnish with the basil and serve.

Honey-Glazed Breast of Duck with Peppercorn Dressing on a Bed of Spiced Celeriac

Noel Cullen/ Reprinted from *Elegant Irish Cooking* (Lebhar-Friedman Books)

Serves 4

While duck used to be cooked and served whole, in recent years, many chefs have started serving just the breast. They generally like to serve it medium rare, which they consider more flavorful than well-done. The honey in this recipe produces a beautiful, dark, and delicious crisp crust.

4 small (2- to 3-ounce) skinless duck breasts
1 teaspoon ground black pepper
3 tablespoons honey
1 tablespoon soy sauce
1 cup chicken stock
1 medium head celeriac
¼ cup (½ stick) butter
1 teaspoon chopped ginger
Salt to taste
4 mint leaves, for garnish

Preheat the oven to 400 degrees F.

Rub the duck breasts with pepper. In a heavy-bottomed ovenproof skillet over high heat, sear the duck breasts on each side, about 2 minutes, depending on the size of the duck breasts. Remove from the skillet and coat with honey.

Return the duck to the skillet. Place the skillet in the oven for 4 minutes. (The center of the duck should be pink).

Remove the duck from the skillet and pour off the fat. Add soy sauce and chicken stock and simmer, reducing slightly to concentrate the flavor. Strain through a fine-mesh sieve.

Peel celeriac and slice into 2-inch-long strips. In a medium saucepan over low heat, melt the butter. Sauté the celeriac with the ginger until tender, about 4 minutes.

Using a 3-inch open ring mold, shape the celeriac on the center of a warmed plate. Slice the duck breast on the bias, and overlay around the celeriac. Pour the combination of pan juices, chicken stock, and soy sauce around the duck. Garnish with mint leaves.

Italian Turkey and Sundried Tomato Sausage

Bruce Aidells and Denis Kelly/Reprinted from *Bruce Aidells' Complete Sausage Book* (Ten Speed Press)

Makes 4 pounds

We were pleased to have on Home Cooking *this year Bruce Aidells, who turned sausage making into an art with recipes like the one below. It's not necessary to always put sausage in a casing, although the sausage-making attachment to the KitchenAid stand mixer makes it very easy and convenient to do so.*

4½ pounds turkey thighs with skin or 4 pounds boneless, with skin and meat separated
4 teaspoons kosher salt
⅓ cup sundried tomatoes
¼ cup white wine
3 tablespoons minced garlic
2 tablespoons fennel seed
1 tablespoon ground pepper
1 teaspoon red pepper
1 teaspoon sugar

When smoking or air-drying sausage, do not dry them in too warm a place. Always hang sausages on clean sticks.

If you have a meat grinder, hand-operated or electric, attach the plate with ⅜-inch holes. Cut the meat into ¾- by ¾-inch wide strips (no larger than the mouth of the grinder), 1 to 6 inches long. While cutting up the meat, take care to remove any gristle and connective tissue. Grind the meat and the skin together into a large bowl. The mixture should come off the grinder plate in "worms." If the meat looks mushy, it means the grinder knife is not making good contact with the plate or the knife is dull. Remove the plate and knife, clean away any gristle, and reassemble, making sure the plate is reasonably tight against the knife. If you continue to have this problem, you might have to buy a new knife.

If you are using a food processor, cut the meat into ¾-inch squares to get reasonably consistent chopping. Process in very small batches of 1 pound or less by using the pulse switch or turning on and off until desired consistency is reached. Do not overprocess the meat. For 4 pounds of meat, you will probably need to process 4 batches. Mini food processors or blenders should not be used to make sausage.

Add all the remaining ingredients. Knead the sausage meat with your hands, squeezing and turning the mixture. Do not overmix, as this could cause the fat to melt and might give the sausage a white, fatty appearance.

Make a small patty of the sausage meat and fry it. Taste and adjust the salt or other seasonings. Cover and refrigerate the meat until you are ready to use in a recipe. Sausage will keep up to 2 days in the refrigerator or 2 months in the freezer.

Sautéed Pork Chops with Wilted Greens, Pine Nuts, and Raisins

Bruce Aidells and Denis Kelly/Reprinted from *The Complete Meat Cookbook* (Houghton Mifflin Company)

Serves 4

Most meats today have approximately 30 percent less fat than they did fifteen years ago and require different cooking approaches, such as the one used in this recipe by Bruce Aidells, which comes from his comprehensive meat cookbook.

4 (1¼ to 1½ inch thick) center cut loin pork chops, either rib or T-bone, trimmed of external fat
Salt and freshly ground black pepper
1 tablespoon olive oil

Pan Sauce and Greens
1 tablespoon olive oil
2 ounces pancetta, diced (optional)
¼ cup finely chopped onion
2 tablespoons chopped garlic
¼ cup chicken or beef stock
4 cups spinach leaves (about 2 bunches)
4 cups coarsely chopped curly endive or Chinese mustard greens (about 2 bunches), without stems
¼ cup golden raisins or sultanas, steeped in boiling water for 5 minutes and drained
1 tablespoon white wine vinegar
¼ cup lightly toasted pine nuts
Salt and freshly ground black pepper

Season the pork chops generously with salt and pepper. In a large heavy skillet, heat the oil over high heat. When the pan is hot enough to sear the chops but not burn them, add the chops. They should make a gentle hissing sound when they hit the pan, not an explosive sputter. Adjust the heat if the pan seems too hot or remove the pan from the heat for 30 seconds or so (count this time as part of the overall cooking time). Sear the chops on one side for 1 to 2 minutes, or until beginning to brown lightly. Turn the chops over and sear for 1 minute more.

Reduce the heat so that the chops continue to sizzle—do not turn the heat so low that there are no more sizzling sounds: If the heat is too low, the chops will sweat and the juices will exude from the meat and leave it dry. Cover the pan and cook for 3 to 4 minutes, depending on how thick the chops are. Turn and cook them for 3 to 4 minutes more on the other side. The chops are done when the meat is firm but not hard when pressed with a finger. Better still, test them with an instant-read thermometer—the meat should measure 145 to 155 degrees F and will still be acceptable at 160 degrees F. For the juiciest results, remove the chops from the pan when they register 145 degrees F, cover loosely with foil, and let them rest for 5 minutes or so before serving, to stabilize the juices. After resting they should read 150 degrees F.

To make the pan sauce and greens, pour off all the fat from the pan. Add the olive oil to the pan and heat over medium heat. If you are using pancetta, sauté it for 5 minutes, stirring often. Remove the pancetta and set it aside; pour off all but 1 tablespoon of the fat. Sauté the onion and garlic in the olive oil or in the remaining tablespoon of fat for about 5 minutes, until the onion is soft. Stir in the stock, scraping any browned bits from the bottom of the pan, and add both kinds of greens. Cover the pan and cook until the greens are wilted, 3 to 4 minutes. Stir in the raisins and cook 1 more minute. Stir in the white wine vinegar and toss the greens to coat them well. Add the pine nuts and the pancetta, if you used it, and toss well in the sauce. Taste for salt and pepper. Serve the chops on the greens.

Grilled Mongolian Lamb with Stir-Fried Vegetables

Robert Clark, Executive Chef at Rain City Grill and C Restaurant

Serves 4

*Robert Clark, one Vancouver's premiere chefs from the Rain City Grill and C Restaurant,
came up with this delicious rack of lamb recipe with its overtone of
Asian flavors. Be sure to cut the vegetables in a uniform dice for even cooking.*

2 whole lamb racks
1 tablespoon sweet soy
3 tablespoons vegetable oil
1 tablespoon black vinegar
1 red bell pepper
1 yellow bell pepper
1 zucchini
1 clove garlic
1 red onion
Salt and pepper
1 tablespoon sesame oil
1 tablespoon rice wine vinegar
1 tablespoon soy sauce
½ cup veal jus

Cut the lamb racks into chops and coat with the soy, 1 tablespoon of the vegetable oil, and vinegar.

Cut all the vegetables into approximately the same size dice. Sweat the onions and garlic in the remaining 2 tablespoons vegetable oil. Add the rest of the vegetables and cook for about 2 minutes. Pour in the remaining ingredients. Bring to a boil and then remove from the heat.

Grill the lamb chops in a grill pan or on a barbecue grill, until desired doneness.

Crunchy Coated Chicken Breasts

Abigail Johnson Dodge/Reprinted from Williams-Sonoma's *The Kid's Cookbook* (Time-Life Books)

Serves 4

This recipe can not only teach kids how to cook, but also entertain them.
Children will have a good time making the cracker crumbs, spreading the mustard,
and rolling the chicken breasts in crumbs.

17 Saltine crackers
¼ cup grated Parmesan cheese
½ teaspoon dried thyme
Salt and pepper
2 tablespoons olive oil
4 (6-ounce) boneless, skinless chicken breast
halves
2 tablespoons Dijon mustard

Preheat the oven to 425 degrees F. Line a jelly-roll pan with aluminum foil and set aside.

Put the crackers in a plastic bag. Press down on the bag to release the air and seal the top. Using a rolling pin, crush the crackers to make coarse crumbs.

Empty the crackers into a shallow bowl. Add the Parmesan cheese, dried thyme, and a good pinch each of salt and pepper. Stir with a table fork until well mixed. Drizzle the olive oil over the crumbs and toss with the fork until the crumbs are evenly moistened.

Rinse the chicken breasts with cold water and pat dry with paper towels. Place them, skinned side up, on a work surface. Spoon the mustard into a small bowl. Using a table knife, spread the mustard over the top of each chicken breast. Sprinkle with salt and pepper.

Press the mustard coated side of the chicken breast half into the crumb mixture. Place the chicken, crumb side up, on the foil-lined jelly-roll pan. Repeat with the other chicken breasts. Sprinkle any leftover crumbs on top of the breasts and pat them onto the chicken with your fingers.

Bake until the chicken is no longer pink in the middle when cut into with a sharp knife, about 25 minutes. Using oven mitts, remove the pan from the oven and serve the chicken immediately.

Scallop and Melon Kebabs

Cheryl Jamison and Bill Jamison/Reprinted from *Born to Grill* (Harvard Common Press)

Makes about 2 dozen kebabs

Master griller Cheryl Jamison, who created this recipe, raved about the combination of scallops and melon. She was right— it's unbeatable. She also warned about overcooking scallops, which can make them tough and dry.

2 pounds sea scallops, halved if larger in diameter than a 50-cent coin
½ cup Peach Vinegar (recipe follows) or other fruit vinegar such as raspberry
1½ teaspoons kosher salt or other coarse salt
1 teaspoon sugar
3 to 4 cups melon balls or bite-sized cubes, from at least 2 types of melon
Soaked bamboo skewers, preferably 2 for each kebab
Vegetable oil spray

Fire up the grill, bringing the temperature to high (1 to 2 seconds with the hand test).

Place the scallops in a plastic bag or shallow bowl and pour the vinegar over them. Let the scallops sit in the vinegar at room temperature for 10 to 20 minutes (much longer and you'll have ceviche). Drain the scallops and discard the vinegar.

Stir the salt and sugar together and sprinkle them lightly over the scallops. Avoiding crowding, skewer 2 to 3 scallops interspersed by balls of different types of melon (preferably using 2 skewers per kebab to hold the ingredients securely while cooking). Assemble the remaining kebabs and spray them lightly with oil.

Transfer the kebabs to a well-oiled grate. Grill them, uncovered, over high heat for 2 to 2½ minutes per side, until the scallops are just opaque with lightly browned edges. Be careful not to overcook or the scallops will become dry and tough. If grilling covered, cook for the same amount of time, turning once midway.

Serve the kebabs immediately.

Peach Vinegar
Makes about 2 cups

2 large peaches, peeled and sliced
2 cups rice vinegar or champagne vinegar

Place the peaches into a large ceramic, glass, or stainless steel bowl and pour the vinegar over them. With the back of a fork, mash the peaches enough to release more juice. Let the mixture sit at room temperature for 6 to 12 hours. Pour through cheesecloth or a fine-mesh strainer into a jar, pushing down with a spoon on the peaches to release more of their flavor. Use the vinegar immediately or store, covered, at room temperature. It keeps for at least several weeks.

Penne with Roasted Tomatoes, Eggplant, and Italian Turkey Sausage

Bruce Aidells and Denis Kelly/Reprinted from *Bruce Aidells' Complete Sausage Book* (Ten Speed Press)

Serves 6

Tomatoes, slow-roasted in a low oven, develop a wonderful flavor. Plum tomatoes with a lower water content work particularly well. We also liked Bruce Aidell's method of roasting eggplant in the oven, which requires less fat than a sauté.

Roasted Tomatoes

2 pounds plum tomatoes, sliced lengthwise into 2 or 3 thick slices

2 tablespoons olive oil

2 tablespoons finely chopped garlic

2 tablespoons chopped fresh herbs, such as basil, oregano, or thyme, or 2 teaspoons dried herbs (use individual herbs or combine)

Salt and freshly ground black pepper

1 large (1½- to 2-pound) unpeeled eggplant, diced

¼ to ½ cup olive oil

Salt and freshly ground black pepper

1 pound Italian Turkey and Sundried Tomato Sausage (page 82) or other mildly spiced sausage removed from casings

12 ounces dried penne or elbow macaroni

½ cup freshly grated Parmesan or Romano cheese

Preheat the oven to 250 degrees F. Spread the sliced tomatoes on baking sheets or roasting pans. Drizzle with olive oil and sprinkle with garlic, herbs, salt, and pepper. Roast until the juices given off by the tomatoes have begun to thicken, about 1 hour. Using a spatula, scrape the tomatoes and all the juices into a non-reactive container.

Increase the oven temperature to 400 degrees F. In a large bowl, toss the eggplant in ¼ cup of the oil and sprinkle with salt and pepper. Spread the eggplant on a baking sheet or roasting pan and bake for 10 minutes. Check the eggplant: If the pieces seem dry, brush with more oil and stir thoroughly. Bake for about 10 minutes more, or until all the eggplant pieces are quite soft and beginning to brown. Remove from the oven and set aside, but do not turn off the oven.

In a large heavy skillet over medium-high heat, heat 2 tablespoons of the olive oil. Add the sausage and cook for 5 minutes, stirring occasionally, leaving the sausage in fairly large pieces. Add the roasted tomatoes and eggplant, season with salt and pepper, and set aside.

Meanwhile, cook the pasta in a large pot of lightly salted boiling water until al dente, 10 to 12 minutes, and drain. Mix together with the pasta sauce and all but 2 tablespoons of the cheese. Spoon the pasta into a shallow baking dish, sprinkle the top with the remaining cheese, and bake until the cheese is golden brown, about 10 minutes. Serve at once.

Glazed Mushroom Pasta

Cheryl Jamison and Bill Jamison/Reprinted from *Born to Grill* (Harvard Common Press)

Serves 6

Here's another ingenious recipe from Cheryl Jamison. After mixing pasta with some meaty, grilled mushrooms and onions, she uses a reduced balsamic vinegar instead of oils and fats as a sauce. The results are scrumptious.

1 pound portobello, porcini, or other meaty wild mushrooms, sliced ⅓ inch thick
½ large red onion, sliced into ⅓-inch-thick rings
2 tablespoons olive oil
½ teaspoon kosher salt or other coarse salt plus more to taste

Mushroom and Onion Glaze
1 cup inexpensive balsamic vinegar
½ teaspoon freshly ground black pepper

1 pound penne or other tube-shaped pasta
1 to 2 tablespoons extra virgin olive oil
3 tablespoons minced fresh parsley

In a medium bowl, toss the mushrooms with the onion, oil, and salt. Let them sit at room temperature while you heat the grill.

Fire up the grill, bringing the temperature to medium (4 to 5 seconds with the hand test).

Prepare the glaze. In a small, heavy saucepan over high heat, boil the vinegar with the pepper until reduced by half.

Grill the mushrooms and onions, uncovered, over medium heat for 8 to 10 minutes, turning occasionally, until the mushrooms are juicy and tender and the onions are crisp-tender. In the last several minutes of cooking, brush the mushrooms and onions on both sides with about two-thirds of the glaze. If grilling covered, cook the mushrooms and onions for 7 to 9 minutes, turning once midway and brushing with the glaze.

Cook the pasta according to the package directions. Slice the onion rings in half and separate them. In a large serving bowl, toss the pasta with the oil and add the mushrooms and onions. Toss again, gently this time, add a little or all of the remaining glaze, and add salt to taste.

Sprinkle with parsley and serve hot or at room temperature.

Creole Braised Chicken with Golden Rice

Marvin Woods/Reprinted from *The New Low-Country Cooking* (William Morrow & Co.)

Serves 6

"Low-country cooking" comes from an eighty-plus-square-mile area surrounding the cities of Charlestown and Savannah and reflects cooking from Africa, France, Spain, and the Caribbean. Once you've made the Creole sauce, which also serves as a base for gumbos and other stews, the dish comes together quickly.

6 chicken legs (thighs and drumsticks)
Salt and freshly ground black pepper
½ cup all-purpose flour
2 tablespoons blended oil, or vegetable or corn oil
1 tablespoon minced garlic
¼ cup minced onion
¼ cup chicken stock
4 cups Creole Sauce (page 94)
Golden Rice (recipe follows)

Place the chicken in a large bowl. Sprinkle it with salt and pepper. Lightly coat the chicken with the flour, shaking off any excess.

Place a large saucepan over medium heat and add the oil. Add the chicken, skin side down, and sear until golden brown, 3 to 5 minutes. Add the garlic and onion and cook, stirring constantly, until softened but not colored, 2 to 3 minutes. Add the stock and Creole Sauce and bring to a boil. Lower the heat and simmer until the chicken pulls away from the bone fairly easily, 45 minutes to 1 hour. Place the rice in a large bowl. Add the chicken and a good amount of the pan juices, and serve.

Golden Rice
Serves 6 to 8

1 tablespoon vegetable oil
½ onion, diced
1 teaspoon saffron threads
1 teaspoon turmeric
2 cups uncooked long-grain white rice
2¼ cups water
1 bay leaf
¾ tablespoon salt

In a large saucepan, heat the oil over medium-high heat. Add the onion and cook, stirring, until transparent, 5 to 7 minutes. Add the saffron, turmeric, and rice and stir together for 1 minute. Add the water, bay leaf, and salt and bring the mixture to a boil. Stir with a fork to prevent the mixture from clumping. Simmer until the grains of rice are tender, about 15 minutes.

Creole Sauce
Makes 6½ cups

3 tablespoons vegetable oil
1½ cups fresh or frozen okra, finely chopped
   (approximately ¾ cup)
1 cup finely chopped celery
1 white onion, finely chopped
1 red bell pepper, seeded and finely chopped
1 green bell pepper, seeded and finely chopped
1 cup fresh or frozen corn kernels
2½ cups vegetable stock
½ cup brown roux
1 cup canned whole plum tomatoes
2 tablespoons hot sauce (your favorite store-
   bought brand)
1½ tablespoons fresh thyme leaves, chopped, or
   2½ teaspoons dried
1½ tablespoons fresh rosemary leaves, chopped
   or 2½ teaspoons dried
1½ tablespoons fresh sage leaves, chopped, or
   2½ teaspoons dried
1 teaspoon chili powder
1 teaspoon cayenne pepper
1 teaspoon chili paste or Thai curry paste
1 tablespoon freshly ground black pepper plus
   more to taste
Salt to taste

In a large soup pot, heat the oil over medium-high heat. Add the okra, celery, onion, bell peppers, and corn and cook, stirring, until the vegetables start to soften, 5 to 7 minutes. Add the vegetable stock and bring the mixture to a slow boil.

When the liquid is boiling, remove about 1 cup and place it in a bowl. Add the brown roux to the 1 cup of stock and stir until it's combined and becomes paste-like. Gradually whisk this mixture back into the simmering liquid. Simmer for 15 minutes.

Add the tomatoes, hot sauce, herbs, chili powder, cayenne, chili paste, and 1 tablespoon black pepper. Taste and check the seasonings, adding salt and pepper if needed. Using a handheld blender, carefully blend all of the ingredients for 30 seconds. (This breaks up the okra and gives the mixture its classic gumbo consistency.) If you do not have a handheld blender, remove 2 cups of the ingredients and process in a blender or food processor. Be careful because the liquid is very hot. Return the purée to the soup pot.

Use the sauce immediately, or cool, cover, and refrigerate for up to 5 to 7 days. You can also freeze it in an airtight container; it will last up to 2 months.

Etta's Pit-Roasted Salmon with Grilled Shiitake Relish

Tom Douglas/Reprinted from *Tom Douglas' Seattle Kitchen* (William Morrow & Co.)

Serves 6

This is a signature dish from chef Tom Douglas's not-to-be-missed restaurant, Etta's Seafood, in Seattle. The secret is its simple rub and the smoky flavors you get from outdoor grilling.

3 tablespoons firmly packed brown sugar
2 tablespoons paprika
2 teaspoons kosher salt
1½ teaspoons freshly ground black pepper
1 teaspoon chopped fresh thyme
6 (7-ounce) salmon fillets
Olive oil
Etta's Cornbread Pudding (recipe follows)
Grilled Shiitake Relish (page 96)
1 lemon, cut into 6 wedges
Fresh basil leaves (optional)

Fire up the grill.

Combine the brown sugar, paprika, salt, pepper, and thyme in a small bowl. Coat both sides of the salmon fillets with all of the rub. (The spice rub can be made a couple days ahead and stored, tightly covered, at room temperature.)

Brush the grill and fish with olive oil. Grill over direct heat, covered, with the vents open. When the salmon is marked by the grill, flip the fish and finish cooking. I like our salmon medium-rare, which requires a total grilling time of around 10 minutes, depending on the heat of the grill. The sugar in the spice rub can burn easily, so watch it closely.

Spoon the warm cornbread pudding onto 6 plates and rest a salmon fillet up against the pudding. Ladle some shiitake relish over each

salmon fillet and garnish with lemon wedges and fresh basil leaves, if desired.

Etta's Cornbread Pudding
Serves 6

Cornbread
1 cup all-purpose flour
¾ cup medium-ground yellow cornmeal
½ cup grated pepper Jack cheese (1½ ounces)
1 teaspoon baking powder
1 teaspoon salt
2 large eggs
1 cup milk
3 tablespoons honey
¼ cup (½ stick) unsalted butter, melted, plus a little more for buttering the pan

Pudding
1 tablespoon unsalted butter, plus a little more for buttering the pan
1 cup thinly sliced onions (about ½ large onion)
¾ cup grated dry Jack cheese
2 teaspoons chopped fresh flat-leaf parsley
½ teaspoon chopped fresh rosemary
½ teaspoon chopped fresh thyme
2¼ cups heavy cream
4 large eggs
1 tablespoon kosher salt
½ teaspoon freshly ground black pepper

Preheat the oven to 425 degrees F. Butter an 8-inch square baking dish. Combine the flour, cornmeal, cheese, baking powder, and salt in a large bowl. In a mixing bowl, whisk together the eggs, milk, and honey. Add the wet ingredients to the dry ingredients, stirring just until combined. Add the melted butter and stir into the mixture. Pour into the prepared pan and bake until a toothpick comes out clean, 15 to 20 minutes. When cool enough to handle, cut into 1-inch cubes. You should have about 8 cups cornbread cubes, but you only need one-third the cornbread cubes (or 2⅔ cups) for this recipe.

To make the pudding, reduce the oven temperature to 350 degrees F. Put the 2⅔ cups of cornbread cubes in a buttered 8-inch square baking dish. Set aside. Heat the 1 tablespoon butter in a sauté pan over low heat and cook the onions very slowly until soft and golden brown, at least 20 minutes, stirring occasionally. Remove from the heat. Scatter the onions, cheese, and herbs over the cornbread cubes. Whisk together the heavy cream and eggs with salt and pepper in a mixing bowl and pour over the cornbread cubes. Let sit for 10 minutes so the cornbread absorbs some of the custard. Bake until set and golden, about 40 minutes. Serve hot.

Note: You can make the cornbread and store it in the freezer, covered tightly with plastic wrap, for a few weeks until you are ready to make the cornbread pudding. The onions can be caramelized a day ahead and stored, covered, in the refrigerator. The cornbread pudding can be baked a day in advance and stored in the refrigerator, covered. Before serving, reheat the cornbread pudding, covered with aluminum foil, in a preheated 375 degree F oven until warmed through, 35 to 40 minutes.

Grilled Shiitake Relish
Serves 4 to 6

¾ **pound fresh shiitake mushroom caps, wiped clean**
3 **tablespoons olive oil**
Kosher salt and freshly ground pepper
2 **tablespoons minced shallots**
2 **teaspoons minced garlic**
½ **teaspoon chopped fresh flat-leaf parsley**
½ **teaspoon chopped fresh sage**
½ **teaspoon chopped fresh rosemary**
½ **teaspoon chopped fresh thyme**
1 **tablespoon balsamic vinegar**
2 **teaspoons fresh lemon juice**

Fire up the grill.

In a bowl, toss the mushroom caps with 2 tablespoons of the oil and sprinkle with salt and pepper. Grill the mushrooms on both sides, over direct heat, until cooked through, about 5 minutes total. Remove the mushrooms from the grill and thinly slice. Heat the remaining 1 tablespoon oil in a sauté pan over medium heat. Add the shallots and garlic and sweat them until soft and aromatic, 2 to 3 minutes. Set aside to cool. In a bowl, combine the mushrooms, shallot-garlic mixture, herbs, vinegar, and lemon juice. Season to taste with salt and pepper. Serve at room temperature.

If you want to make this relish and you are not planning to grill, you could roast the mushrooms instead. Toss the mushrooms with the oil, salt, and pepper, then spread them on a baking sheet. Roast them in a preheated 450 degree F oven for 20 minutes.

Ricotta Gnocchi with Proscuitto and Porcini Mushroom Sauce (Gnocchi con Sugo di Prosciutto e Funghi Porcini)

Biba Caggiano/Reprinted from *Biba's Taste of Italy* (HarperCollins Publishers)

Serves 4 to 6

Most people are familiar with gnocchi made from potatoes, but this is a wonderful version made with ricotta cheese. Together with the porcini mushroom sauce, the dish lifts you up and takes you right to Italy.

Sauce
1 ounce dried porcini mushrooms, soaked in 2
   cups lukewarm water for 20 minutes
1 heaping teaspoon double-concentrated Italian
   tomato paste
2 tablespoons unsalted butter
2 tablespoons extra virgin olive oil
²/₃ cup finely minced yellow onions
1 clove garlic, finely minced
¼ pound prosciutto, in 1 thick slice, finely diced
½ cup dry white wine
Salt and freshly ground black pepper to taste

1 tablespoon coarse salt
1 recipe Ricotta Gnocchi (recipe follows)
½ cup freshly grated Parmigiano-Reggiano

To prepare the sauce, drain the porcini mushrooms and reserve the soaking water. Rinse the mushrooms well under cold running water and roughly chop them; set aside. Line a strainer with paper towels and strain the soaking liquid into a bowl. Pour 1½ cups of the strained liquid into a small bowl, stir in the tomato paste, and set aside.

Heat 1 tablespoon of the butter and the oil together in a large skillet over medium heat. When the butter begins to foam, add the onions and cook, stirring, until lightly golden and soft, 5 to 6 minutes. Add the garlic, porcini, and prosciutto and stir for 1 to 2 minutes. Raise the heat to high and add the wine. Cook, stirring

briskly, until the wine is reduced by approximately half. Add the diluted tomato paste, season with salt and pepper, and reduce the heat to medium-low. Simmer, uncovered, stirring occasionally, until the sauce has a medium-thick consistency, 12 to 15 minutes. Taste and adjust the seasoning. (Makes about 1½ cups.) The sauce can be prepared several hours ahead. Reheat gently before proceeding.

While the sauce is cooking, bring a large pot of water to a boil over high heat. Add the coarse salt and the gnocchi and cook until the gnocchi rise to the surface, 1 to 2 minutes. After 20 to 30 seconds, remove the gnocchi with a slotted spoon or a skimmer, draining the excess water back into the pot, and place the gnocchi in the skillet with the sauce.

Add the remaining 1 tablespoon butter and about half of the Parmigiano. Mix well over medium heat until the gnocchi and sauce are well combined. Taste, adjust the seasoning, and serve with the remaining Parmigiano.

Ricotta Gnocchi (Gnocchi di Ricotta)
Serves 4 to 6

1 pound whole-milk ricotta
⅓ cup freshly grated Parmigiano-Reggiano
4 teaspoons salt
1 large egg, beaten
1 to 1½ cups unbleached all-purpose flour

To make the dough, combine the ricotta, Parmigiano, 2 teaspoons of the salt, and 1 cup of the flour in a large bowl. Mix together well with your hands until the ingredients are evenly blended and the mixture comes together into a rough dough.

Transfer the dough to a wooden board or other work surface and knead lightly, gradually adding the remaining ½ cup flour if the dough sticks too much to the board and your hands. Then knead the dough for 2 to 3 minutes, dusting lightly with flour if needed, until it is smooth, pliable, and just a bit sticky.

To shape the gnocchi, cut off a piece of dough about the size of an orange. Flour your hands lightly (do not flour the work surface, or the dough will not slide smoothly.) Using both hands, roll out a piece of dough with a light back-and-forth motion into a rope about the thickness of your index finger. Cut the rope into 1-inch pieces.

Hold a fork with the tines against the work surface, the curved part of the fork facing away from you. Starting from the bottom of the tines of the fork, press each piece of dough with your index finger firmly upward along the length of the tines, then let the gnocchi fall back onto the work surface. Repeat with the remaining dough until all gnocchi have been formed.

Line a large tray with a clean kitchen towel and flour the towel lightly. Place the gnocchi on the towel, without crowding them. They can be cooked immediately or be refrigerated, uncovered, for several hours.

To cook the gnocchi, bring a large pot of water to a boil over high heat. Add the remaining 2 teaspoons salt and the gnocchi and cook until all the gnocchi rise to the surface, 1 to 2 minutes. After 20 to 30 seconds, remove the gnocchi with a slotted spoon or a skimmer, draining the excess water back into the pot, and place in the sauce or a heated bowl.

Pasta with Sundried Tomatoes and Mushrooms

Michael Lomonaco/Reprinted from *The '21' Cookbook* (Doubleday)

Serves 4

Here's a classic pasta dish that should be in everyone's cooking repertoire. The pine nuts, also referred to as pignoli, are actually found inside pinecones. It's a time-consuming process to remove them, which is why they are sometimes costly.

6 to 8 quarts water
2 tablespoons salt
¼ cup fresh basil leaves
1 pound dried pasta, such as fettucine, or Fresh Pasta (recipe follows)
3 tablespoons pine nuts
½ pound assorted mushrooms, such as shiitake, oyster, and cremini, cleaned and sliced
½ cup sundried tomatoes, soaked in 1 cup hot water 30 minutes, then drained and julienned
¼ cup extra virgin olive oil
1 tablespoon chopped garlic
¼ teaspoon crushed red pepper flakes
¼ cup freshly grated Parmesan cheese
Salt and freshly ground black pepper to taste

Preheat the oven to 350 degrees F. Bring the water to a rolling boil in a large pot and add the salt. Meanwhile, stack the basil leaves and slice into julienne strips using a sharp knife so that you don't bruise the basil and cause it to blacken. Set aside. Add the pasta to the boiling water. Place the pine nuts on a cookie sheet and bake until slightly browned. Sauté the mushrooms and tomatoes in the olive oil. Remove from the heat and add the basil, garlic, red pepper, half the pine nuts and cheese, and salt and pepper to taste.

When the pasta is al dente, drain and toss with the mushroom/tomato/herb mixture. Divide among 4 plates and garnish each serving with the remaining pine nuts and cheese.

Fresh Pasta
Serves 6

3 cups all-purpose flour
1½ teaspoons salt
3 eggs, slightly beaten
¼ cup water plus 2 tablespoons, if needed

In a medium-sized bowl, combine flour and salt. Make a well in the flour, add the slightly beaten egg and ¼ cup water, and mix. This mixture should form a stiff dough. If needed, stir in 1 to 2 tablespoons water.

Turn the dough out onto a lightly floured surface and knead for about 3 to 4 minutes. With a pasta machine or by hand, roll dough out to desired thinness. Use the machine or a knife to cut into strips of desired width.

Star Anise Game Hens

Tom Douglas/Reprinted from *Tom Douglas' Seattle Kitchen* (William Morrow & Co.)

Serves 2 to 4

*Caramelized sugar gives these hens a beautiful golden color while the ginger,
along with the other Asian ingredients, gives them an extraordinary flavor. Use extreme
caution when working with the caramelized sugar.*

2 (1½-pound) Cornish game hens

Star Anise Marinade
¾ **cup sugar**
¼ **cup water**
1 cup sake
Zest from 1 orange, cut with a peeler into
  ½-inch-wide strips
3 star anise, crushed with a rolling pin
2 tablespoons peeled and grated fresh ginger
⅓ **cup soy sauce**
¼ **cup Asian fish sauce**
⅓ **cup honey**
⅓ **cup peanut or vegetable oil**

Aromatic steamed rice

Trim any excess fat from the Cornish game hens. Cut out the backbones and split the hens in half through the breastbones. Place in a nonreactive baking pan and refrigerate.

To make the marinade, in a heavy-bottomed saucepan over medium-low heat, combine the sugar and water, stirring until the sugar completely dissolves. Raise the heat to high and cook, undisturbed, until the sugar caramelizes to a golden brown color, 5 to 8 minutes. As soon as the sugar is caramelized, remove the saucepan from the heat and add the sake. Be careful because the mixture will sputter. When the mixture settles, return the saucepan to medium-low heat and stir until any hardened strands of caramel melt.

Remove the saucepan from the heat and pour the caramel syrup into a bowl. Stir in the zest, star anise, ginger, and soy and fish sauces. Whisk in the honey and oil. Allow the marinade to cool. Reserve 1 cup of the marinade, then pour the rest over the game hens, turning them in the marinade to coat completely. Cover with plastic wrap and refrigerate overnight.

Preheat the oven to 375 degrees F. Set aside ½ cup of the reserved marinade for basting and pour the rest into ramekins for serving with the hens. Remove the game hens from the marinade and place them on a baking sheet. (For easier cleanup, line the baking sheet with aluminum foil because the excess marinade will drip off and burn.) Roast the hens in the oven for 25 to 30 minutes, basting with the reserved marinade occasionally, until the hens are cooked through. An instant-read thermometer inserted into the thickest part of the thigh should read 165 degrees F and the juices should run clear from the cavity and the thigh when sliced into. Remove the hens from the oven and preheat the broiler. Place the hens under the broiler for 1 to 2 minutes to caramelize the glaze, turning the baking pan as needed. Watch carefully because the glaze burns easily.

Place 1 or 2 game hen halves on each plate next to a mound of the rice. Serve with the ramekins of reserved marinade.

Note: The marinade can be made a few days ahead and stored, covered, in the refrigerator.

Seared Salmon Fillets

Pam Anderson/Reprinted from *How to Cook without a Book* (Broadway Books)

Serves 4

The technique of searing involves high heat, so make sure your pan is very hot before adding the food. It's also important to choose the right size pan. If it's too small, the food will be overcrowded and will steam instead of sear; if it's too large, the excess pan space will smoke.

4 (6-ounce) center-cut salmon fillets
2 tablespoons olive oil
Salt and ground black pepper
Lemon wedges, or a pan sauce, uncooked relish, or flavored butter

Set a heavy-bottomed 12-inch skillet over low heat for 5 to 10 minutes, or medium heat for 3 to 4 minutes, while preparing the meal and seasoning the salmon. Three to four minutes before searing the salmon, turn on the exhaust fan and increase the heat to high.

Set the fillets on a plate, drizzle with oil; turn to coat. Sprinkle both sides with salt and pepper.

A minute or so after the residual oils in the skillet send up a wisp of smoke, put the salmon fillets, flesh side down, in the pan. Cook over high heat until they develop an even rich brown crust, 3 to 3 ½ minutes. Turn the fillets and continue to cook until the skin side develops an even, rich brown crust, 4 minutes longer for medium and 5 minutes longer for medium-well. Remove to a plate and let stand for a few minutes or while making a sauce.

Serve with lemon wedges, or an uncooked relish or flavored butter. Or make a pan sauce (see page 111) by adding ½ cup liquid to the skillet; boil until the liquid is reduced to about ¼ cup. Tilting the skillet so that the reduced liquid is at one side of the pan, whisk in butter or other enrichments until the sauce is smooth and glossy.

Weeknight Stir-Fry

Pam Anderson/Reprinted from *How to Cook without a Book* (Broadway Books)

Serves 4

*Pam Anderson's unique book teaches people the principles behind basic cooking techniques so
they can be free to invent their own recipes or use ingredients they have on hand. In this stir-fry recipe,
it's your choice whether you go with chicken, beef, or meatless.*

1 pound beef, pork, poultry, seafood, or tofu (see recipes that follow), cut into bite-sized pieces

1 tablespoon soy sauce

1 tablespoon dry sherry

1 medium-large onion (about 8 ounces), halved from pole to pole, each half cut into 8 wedges

1 pound vegetables (see recipes that follow), cut into approximate size of the selected meat or seafood

1 tablespoon minced garlic

1 tablespoon minced ginger

1 recipe flavoring sauce (see pages 111)

2 teaspoons cornstarch mixed with 2 tablespoons canned chicken broth, plus extra if necessary

3 tablespoons peanut or vegetable oil

Heat a skillet over low heat while preparing stir-fry ingredients. Three or four minutes before stir-frying, increase the heat to high.

Toss the protein of choice with the soy sauce and sherry in a medium bowl. Place the onion and vegetables in a medium-large bowl and keep separate. Place the garlic and ginger in a small bowl and set aside. Place the flavoring sauce and cornstarch mixed with chicken broth in small bowls and set aside.

When ready to stir-fry, drizzle 1 tablespoon of the oil to coat the pan completely. Add half the protein of choice; stir-fry until seared and just cooked through, 2 to 3 minutes. Transfer to a clean bowl. Stir-fry the remaining protein, adding it to the bowl when cooked.

Drizzle the remaining oil (1½ to 2 tablespoons) into the hot skillet. Add the onion; stir-fry until browned but still crisp, about 1 minute. Add the garlic and ginger, then the second vegetable; continue to stir-fry until softened but still crisp, 1 to 2 minutes longer. Add the final vegetable; sauté until all vegetables are tender-crisp, 1 to 2 minutes longer. Return the protein to the pan.

Stir in the flavoring sauce; stir-fry to coat all ingredients. Stir in the cornstarch mixture and add to the skillet; stir until the juices become saucy and glossy. If the pan juices look too thick, add a couple more tablespoons chicken broth. Serve immediately.

Stir-Fried Chicken with Baby Corn and Zucchini
Serves 4

Protein
1 pound skinless, boneless chicken breasts or
    thighs, cut crosswise into bite-sized chunks

Vegetables
8 ounces zucchini, cut into $\frac{1}{2}$-inch-thick rounds or
    julienne strips 2 inches long and $\frac{1}{4}$ inch thick
1 (14-ounce) can baby corn, drained and rinsed

Flavoring Sauce
1 recipe Basil (or Cilantro) Flavoring Sauce
    (page 111)

Follow the Weeknight Stir-Fry recipe (page 106),
adding the zucchini to the skillet before the
corn.

Stir-Fried Beef with Celery and Water Chestnuts
Serves 4

3 cups all-purpose flour
$1\frac{1}{2}$ teaspoons salt
3 eggs, slightly beaten
$\frac{1}{4}$ cup water plus 2 tablespoons, if needed

Protein
$\frac{3}{4}$ to 1 pound flank steak, sliced thin on a slight
    angle, or other steak, sliced thin

Vegetables
10 to 12 ounces celery, trimmed and sliced
    crosswise $\frac{1}{4}$ inch thick
1 (8-ounce) can water chestnuts (drained weight
    5 ounces), rinsed

Flavoring Sauce
1 recipe Soy-Sesame Flavoring Sauce (page 111)

Follow the Weeknight Stir-Fry recipe (page 106),
adding celery to the skillet before the water
chestnuts.

Stir-Fried Chicken, Snow Peas, and Water Chestnuts

Serves 4

Protein

¾ to 1 pound skinless, boneless chicken breasts
   or thighs, cut into bite-sized strips or chunks

Vegetables

½ pound snow peas, strings removed
1 (8-ounce) can sliced water chestnuts (drained
   weight 5 ounces)

Flavoring Sauce

1 recipe Lemon Flavoring Sauce (page 111)

Follow the Weeknight Stir-Fry recipe (page 106),
adding snow peas to the skillet before the water
chestnuts.

Stir-Fry Sauces

Lemon Flavoring Sauce

¼ cup lemon juice plus 1 teaspoon lemon zest
¼ cup canned chicken broth
1 tablespoon soy sauce
2 tablespoons sugar

Mix all ingredients in a small bowl and set aside.

Sweet-and-Sour Flavoring Sauce

¼ cup canned chicken broth
2 tablespoons soy sauce
2 tablespoons cider, balsamic, or rice wine vinegar
1 tablespoon brown sugar
½ teaspoon crushed red pepper flakes

Mix all ingredients in a small bowl and set aside.

Basil (or Cilantro) Flavoring Sauce

¼ cup canned chicken broth
¼ cup soy sauce
2 teaspoons rice wine vinegar
½ teaspoon sugar
¼ cup shredded fresh basil leaves or chopped
   fresh cilantro

Mix all ingredients in a small bowl and set aside.

Soy-Sesame Flavoring Sauce

¼ cup canned low-sodium chicken broth
¼ cup soy sauce
2 teaspoons rice wine vinegar
2 teaspoons toasted sesame oil
1 teaspoon crushed red pepper flakes
1 teaspoon sugar

Mix all ingredients in a small bowl and set aside.

Pan Sauces

Lemon-Caper Pan Sauce
6 tablespoons low-sodium chicken broth
2 tablespoons lemon juice
2 teaspoons drained capers
1 tablespoon butter

Combine the broth, lemon juice, and capers in a measuring cup. Follow instructions for making a pan sauce in individual recipes.

Orange-Dijon Pan Sauce with Rosemary
½ cup orange juice
1 teaspoon Dijon mustard
½ teaspoon minced fresh rosemary leaves
1 tablespoon butter

Combine the orange juice, mustard, and rosemary in a measuring cup. Follow instructions for making a pan sauce in individual recipes.

Curried Chutney Pan Sauce
6 tablespoons canned low-sodium chicken broth
2 tablespoons rice wine vinegar
2 tablespoons prepared chutney, such as Major
   Grey's
¼ teaspoon curry powder
1 tablespoon butter

Combine the broth and vinegar with the chutney and curry powder. Follow instructions for making a pan sauce in individual recipe.

Sautéed Boneless, Skinless Chicken Cutlets

Pam Anderson/Reprinted from *How to Cook without a Book* (Broadway Books)

Serves 4

Most people love the results of a good chicken sauté—a golden brown finish that protects the succulent, perfectly cooked chicken. Be sure to use a medium-high heat for best results. The drippings in the pan are the base of a number of delicious sauces, like the ones in this recipe.

2 tablespoons butter

1 tablespoon oil

4 boneless chicken breast halves, trimmed of fat and tenderloins removed, and pounded with the dull side of a chef's knife until more or less textured

Salt and ground black pepper

¼ cup flour measured into a pie plate or other shallow pan

Lemon wedges, or a pan sauce or uncooked relish

Heat the butter and oil in an 11- to 12-inch skillet over low heat. While the pan is heating, sprinkle the chicken breasts and tenderloins on both sides with salt and pepper, then dredge in flour.

A couple of minutes before sautéing, increase the heat to medium-high. When the butter stops foaming and starts to smell nutty, arrange the chicken breasts, skin side up, and tenderloins in the skillet. Cook, turning only once, until the chicken breasts are rich golden brown, about 3 minutes per side (tenderloins will be done a little sooner). Remove the chicken from the skillet.

Serve immediately with lemon wedges or an uncooked relish. Or make a pan sauce (see page 111) by adding ½ cup liquid to the skillet; boil until the liquid is reduced to about ¼ cup. Tilting the skillet so that the reduced liquid is at one side of the pan, whisk in butter or other enrichments until the sauce is smooth and glossy. Spoon a portion of the sauce over each sautéed chicken breast and serve immediately.

Cedar-Planked Salmon Fillets with Shallot and Dill Crust

Ted Reader and Kathleen Sloan/Reprinted from *The Sticks and Stones Cookbook* (Macmillan Canada)

Serves 8

North American Indians discovered the wonderful flavor salmon picks up when cooked on a cedar plank. You can purchase cedar planks at nearly any hardware store, but be sure to get ones that are untreated.

8 skinless fillets of Atlantic salmon, about
   2 inches thick (6 ounces each)
Sea salt
1 cup chopped fresh dill
½ cup chopped shallots
2 cloves garlic, chopped
2 scallions, chopped
3 tablespoons cracked black pepper
Juice of 1 lemon
1 tablespoon Bone Dust Barbecue Spice
   (recipe follows)
2 tablespoons olive oil
2 cedar planks, soaked in water for at least
   12 hours
1 large lemon for squeezing

Preheat grill to high.

Season salmon fillets with sea salt and set to one side. In a bowl, combine the dill, shallots, garlic, scallions, black pepper, lemon juice, Bone Dust Barbecue Spice, and olive oil. Blend together well. Use this mixture to form a crust on the flesh side (not the skin side) of each salmon fillet.

Season soaked planks with sea salt and place on the grill; close the lid and heat for 3 to 5 minutes until they start to crackle and smoke. Carefully lift the lid and place salmon fillets on the hot planks, skin side down. Close the lid and plank-bake salmon for 12 to 15 minutes (medium doneness). Check periodically to make sure that the planks are not on fire. Use a spray bottle to extinguish any flames. Squeeze lemon over the fillets. Carefully remove the planks from the grill, and using a metal spatula, transfer salmon fillets to a serving platter. Serve immediately.

Bone Dust Barbecue Spice
Makes approximately 2½ cups

½ cup paprika
¼ cup chili powder
3 tablespoons salt
2 tablespoons ground coriander
2 tablespoons garlic powder
2 tablespoons granulated sugar
2 tablespoons curry powder
2 tablespoons dry hot mustard
1 tablespoon freshly ground black pepper
1 tablespoon ground basil
1 tablespoon ground thyme
1 tablespoon ground cumin
1 tablespoon cayenne

In a bowl, mix all ingredients together well. Store in a tightly sealed container.

Roasted Stuffed Turkey Breast (Arrosto di Tacchino Farcito)

Biba Caggiano/Reprinted from *Biba's Taste of Italy* (HarperCollins Publishers)

Serves 8

This is a wonderful main dish for a dinner party. After the turkey breast is rolled with its spinach and mortadella filling, then cooked and sliced, the results are beautiful pinwheels that taste as good as they look.

1 pound spinach, stems and bruised leaves discarded, or 1 (10-ounce) package frozen spinach, thawed and squeezed dry

Salt

4 tablespoons unsalted butter

2 to 3 tablespoons heavy cream

¼ cup freshly grated Parmigiano-Reggiano

1 (4- to 4½-pound) boneless turkey breast, butterflied and pounded thin by the butcher

Freshly ground black pepper to taste

10 thin slices mortadella, prosciutto, or baked ham (about ½ pound)

2 tablespoons extra virgin olive oil

1 to 2 cups dry white wine

If using fresh spinach, wash it thoroughly under cold running water, then put 2 cups water, a nice pinch of salt, and the spinach in a large pot and bring to a gentle boil. Cover the pot and cook, stirring a few times, until the spinach is tender, 6 to 8 minutes. Drain the spinach and squeeze out the excess water.

Place the fresh or frozen spinach on a cutting board and chop very fine.

Melt 2 tablespoons of the butter in a medium skillet over medium heat. When the butter begins to foam, add the spinach, cream, and Parmigiano and season lightly with salt. Stir for 1 to 2 minutes, until the cheese has melted and the cream and Parmigiano coat the spinach. Transfer to a bowl and let cool.

Preheat the oven to 375 degrees F.

Place the turkey breast skin side down on a work surface and season with salt and pepper. Cover the turkey with slices of mortadella, leaving a 2-inch border all around. With a tablespoon or a spatula, spread the spinach mixture over the mortadella. Top the spinach with the remaining slices of mortadella. Starting from a long side, roll up the turkey breast tightly and tie securely with kitchen string. Season the roast with salt and pepper. (The turkey can be prepared up to this point several hours ahead. Cover with plastic wrap and refrigerate.)

Heat the remaining 2 tablespoons butter and the oil in a large heavy casserole over medium heat. Add the turkey and cook, turning, until golden on all sides, 8 to 10 minutes. Add 1 cup of the wine and bring to a boil. Let the wine bubble for a minute or so, then transfer the casserole to the center rack of the oven. Roast the turkey for about 1 hour, basting every 20 minutes or so with its pan juices. Add a bit more wine if the sauce in the pan reduces too much. To test the turkey for doneness, pierce it with a long thin knife: If the juices run clear, the turkey is done. Transfer the roast to a cutting board and let it rest for 5 to 10 minutes while you finish the sauce.

Set the pot over high heat and bring the pan juices to a boil. Add a bit more wine or water if needed. Stir quickly with a wooden spoon, scraping the pot to loosen the browned bits on the bottom. When the juices are nicely thickened, turn off the heat.

Remove the string, slice the turkey, and serve with a drizzle of sauce.

Note: To enrich the taste of the pan juices, stir in 3 to 4 tablespoons balsamic vinegar after they have thickened.

Sautéed Chicken Breasts with Oven-Dried Grapes

Rozanne Gold/Reprinted from *Healthy 1 - 2 - 3* (Stewart Tabori & Chang)

Serves 4

At first glance, you may think the recipe is missing some ingredients, but the list is complete. A total of three ingredients is the signature and brilliance of Rozanne Gold's recipes, which always have stunningly simple and delicious results.

1½ pounds seedless grapes: ¾ pound red, ¾ pound green
3½ tablespoons unsalted butter, chilled
4 (6-ounce) skinless, boneless chicken breasts
Kosher salt and freshly ground black pepper

Preheat the oven to 275 degrees F.

Wash the grapes and remove the stems. Set aside half of the red and half of the green grapes. Place the remaining grapes on a baking sheet and bake for 1½ hours, shaking the pan frequently. Remove from the oven and set aside.

Place uncooked grapes in a blender and purée until very smooth. Strain through a coarse-mesh sieve, pressing down hard on the skins. You will have about ¾ cup juice.

In a large nonstick skillet, melt 2 tablespoons butter. Season the chicken with kosher salt and freshly ground black pepper. Add to the pan and cook over medium-high heat for 5 minutes on each side, until golden.

Add the grape juice and cook for 5 minutes longer, or until the chicken is done and is just firm to the touch. Be careful not to overcook. The grape juices will darken into a mahogany-colored sauce. Transfer the breasts to a platter.

Add the remaining 1½ tablespoons butter to the pan and cook over high heat for 1 minute. Add the oven-dried grapes and cook for 1 minute longer. Add salt and pepper to taste and pour the sauce over the chicken. Serve immediately.

Tagliata di Manzo (Sliced Grilled Steak)

Editors of *Saveur* Magazine/Reprinted from *Saveur Cooks Authentic Italian* (Chronicle Books)

Serves 4

This recipe comes from the grande dame *of Italian cooking, Marcella Hazan. Simple on the surface, its distinctive character comes from its liberal use of garlic and rosemary and the novel technique of cooking the steak twice.*

½ cup extra-virgin olive oil
12 cloves garlic
2 sprigs fresh rosemary
2 boneless rib-eye or strip steaks, 2 inches thick
Salt and freshly ground black pepper

Heat oil and garlic in a medium sauté pan over medium-high heat. Cook, stirring occasionally, until garlic is pale gold, about 7 minutes. Remove from the heat and add rosemary sprigs, turning them over several times, then set pan (with garlic and rosemary) aside.

Heat a large cast-iron skillet or stovetop grill over high heat. When the skillet is very hot, add steaks, which should sizzle instantly and quickly begin to smoke. Cook until very brown on one side, 2 to 3 minutes, then turn steaks over, sprinkle with salt, and cook for another 3 minutes (the steaks should be very rare).

Remove the skillet from the heat and transfer the steaks to a cutting board. Slice them on an angle, across the grain, into ½-inch-thick slices.

Return the pan with the garlic and rosemary to the stove and heat over medium-high heat. When the oil begins to heat up, add the steak slices, together with any juices from the cutting board. Cook for about 1 minute, turning frequently and seasoning generously with black pepper. Adjust salt if necessary.

Butter-Rubbed Roast Turkey with an Apple Cider Glaze

Diane Morgan/Reprinted from *The Thanksgiving Table* (Chronicle Books)

Serves 12 to 20, depending on the size of the turkey

Brining is really worth the time and effort, especially for such an important meal as Thanksgiving.
It gives the food extra flavor and the meat comes out moist and succulent.

1 large yellow onion (about 10 ounces), quartered
4 cloves garlic
2 Golden Delicious apples, cored and quartered
4 sprigs fresh thyme
4 fresh sage leaves
1 Brined Turkey (12–16 pounds) made with Apple Cider Brine (recipes follow)
½ cup (1 stick) unsalted butter, melted
2 teaspoons kosher salt
Freshly ground pepper
Turkey giblets (neck, tail, gizzard, and heart)
1 cup homemade chicken stock or canned low-sodium chicken broth
2 cups unsweetened apple cider or juice
2 tablespoons all-purpose flour

Position an oven rack on the second lowest level in the oven. Preheat the oven to 500 degrees F. Have ready a large roasting pan with a roasting rack, preferably V-shaped, set in the pan.

Place the onion, garlic, apples, thyme, and sage inside the chest cavity of the turkey. Truss the turkey. Use a pastry brush to brush the turkey with the butter. Season the turkey with salt and a few grinds of freshly ground pepper. Place the turkey, breast side down, on a roasting rack. Add the giblets, stock, and 1 cup of the apple cider to the pan. Roast for 30 minutes. Lower the oven temperature to 350 degrees F. Baste the turkey with the pan juices, and roast an additional 30 minutes. Remove the turkey from the oven. Use

oven mitts covered with aluminum foil, or wads of paper towels, and turn the turkey breast side up. Baste with the pan juices, then return the turkey to the oven.

Continue to roast the turkey, basting occasionally. After it has roasted for 2 hours, begin basting every 30 minutes with the remaining 1 cup of apple cider. The turkey is done when an instant-read thermometer reads 165 degrees F when inserted into the thickest part of the thigh. When an internal temperature of the turkey is 125 degrees F, the turkey is about 1 hour away from being done. (Roasting times will vary depending on the size of the bird, its temperature when it went into the oven, whether or not it is stuffed, and your particular oven and the accuracy of the thermostat.)

When the turkey is done, transfer it to a carving board or serving platter, and cover the breast loosely with aluminum foil. Allow the turkey to rest for 15 to 30 minutes before carving to let the juices set.

While the turkey is resting, make the gravy. Place the roasting pan over medium-high heat. Discard the giblets. Skim any fat from the surface, and bring the liquid in the pan to a simmer. Using a wooden spoon, scrape and loosen any browned bits sticking to the bottom and sides of the pan. Place the flour in a 1-cup measure, add a small amount of the simmering liquid, and blend until smooth. Slowly pour this into the simmering liquid and whisk until thickened, about 3 minutes. Season to taste with salt and pepper. Transfer to a small bowl or sauceboat and serve with the turkey.

Brined Turkey

1 fresh or thawed turkey (10 to 25 pounds)
2 oranges, quartered
Apple Cider Brine (recipe follows)

Have ready a heavy roasting pan large enough to hold the turkey and 2 turkey-sized plastic oven bags. Place a plastic oven bag inside the other one to create a double thickness; then place these bags, open wide, in the roasting pan. Remove the turkey from its wrapping. Remove the neck and bag of giblets from the main and neck cavity of the bird. Store separately in the refrigerator for making gravy. Stuff the main cavity of the turkey with the orange quarters.

Fold back the top third of the bags, making a collar (this helps to keep the top of the bag open). Place the turkey inside the double-thick bags, stand it upright, unfold the top of the bag, and pour the Apple Cider Brine over the bird. Add 2 cups cold water. Squeeze out as much air as possible from the inner bag; then close it with a twist tie. Do the same for the outer bag. Place the turkey, breast side down, in the roasting pan and refrigerate for 12 to 24 hours. Turn the turkey 3 or 4 times while it is brining.

Just prior to roasting, remove the turkey from the brine. Discard the bags, brine, and any cured herbs or spices remaining on the bird. Discard the oranges and ginger. Rinse the turkey under cold water and pat dry with paper towels.

Apple Cider Brine
Makes 3½ quarts brine

⅔ cup kosher salt
⅔ cup sugar
6 quarter-sized slices fresh ginger
2 bay leaves
6 whole cloves
1 teaspoon black peppercorns, crushed
2 teaspoons whole allspice berries, crushed
2 quarts unsweetened apple cider or juice

In a 3- to 4-quart saucepan, put all the ingredients and stir to combine. Bring to a boil over medium-high heat, stirring until the salt and sugar have dissolved. Boil for 3 minutes; then remove from the heat. Add 4 cups of ice-cold water, stir, and set aside to cool. Then proceed with the directions for Brined Turkey.

Lacquered Salmon, Pineapple-Soy Reduction

Rozanne Gold/Reprinted from *Healthy 1 - 2 - 3* (Stewart Tabori & Chang)

Serves 4

Here is another ingenious three-ingredient recipe from Rozanne Gold,
which comes out with a beautiful finish and delightful taste.

2 cups unsweetened pineapple juice
4 teaspoons Japanese shoyu or tamari (see Note)
4 (6½-ounce) thick salmon steaks

Put pineapple juice in a small nonreactive saucepan. Bring to a boil. Lower heat to medium and cook until the juice is reduced to 1 cup. Transfer to a small bowl and let cool.

Mix shoyu with reduced pineapple juice.

Place salmon in a shallow casserole. Pour the pineapple-soy mixture over the fish. Refrigerate and marinate for 2 hours, turning after 1 hour.

Heat a large nonstick skillet or 2 smaller non-stick skillets until hot. Sear fish for 3 minutes on each side or until cooked through. Be careful not to overcook.

Meanwhile, place the remaining pineapple-shoyu mixture in a small saucepan and cook over medium-low heat until reduced by half, about 5 minutes. Using a pastry brush, glaze the top of the salmon with a little of the reduced marinade and remove salmon from the pan. Serve each portion with some of the remaining marinade. Serve immediately.

Note: Traditional Japanese soy sauce, or shoyu, is made from fermented soybeans, wheat, and salt, and has a highly complex flavor. Commercial brands—made usually with hydrolyzed vegetable protein, salt, flavorings, and caramel flavor—are not good substitutes. Tamari, usually made without wheat, is a bit heavier, but quite acceptable.

Pan-Fried Catskill Trout with Wild Mushrooms and Asparagus

Michael Lomonaco

Serves 4

Here's a delicious way to dress up trout, including a finishing sauce that's delectable and easy to make. Don't fret about your fish boning skills—let your fishmonger butterfly the trout for you—then it's sheer enjoyment putting the dish together.

4 (8- to 10-ounce) fresh butterflied rainbow trout
Salt and freshly ground pepper to taste
4 tablespoons olive oil
½ pound exotic or wild mushrooms, such as morels, cleaned carefully and quartered
3 shallots, finely chopped
¾ pound young, thin asparagus tips and stems, trimmed
½ cup fish stock
¼ cup dry white wine
3 tablespoons chopped fresh thyme
3 tablespoons unsalted butter

Season the trout with salt and pepper inside and out. Heat 2 tablespoons olive oil over medium heat in a large 12-inch skillet for 30 seconds. Add the trout and sauté the filleted fish for 2½ to 3 minutes on each side, before removing from the pan and placing onto a serving platter. Keep warm.

Using the same sauté pan as the fish were cooked in, add the remaining olive oil and heat for several seconds before adding the cleaned mushrooms. Cook the mushrooms for 2 minutes before adding the shallots and continue to cook for 2 to 3 minutes more. Add the asparagus to the mushrooms and cook together for 1 minute. Add the fish stock and white wine and allow the vegetables to braise in this liquid for 2 minutes. Add the thyme and swirl in the butter. Remove promptly from the heat and allow the butter (which adds a creamy texture to the dish) to melt. Spoon over the fish and serve promptly.

Yakitori Chicken

Jamie Purviance and Sandra S. McRae/Reprinted from *Weber's Big Book of Grilling* (Chronicle Books)

Serves 4 to 6

Yakitori *means "grilled fowl" in Japanese and is one of the cuisine's most popular dishes. Be careful not to overcook the chicken breast so it stays moist and juicy.*

Marinade
3/4 **cup soy sauce**
1/2 **cup mirin (sweet rice wine)**
1/4 **cup ketchup**
2 **tablespoons rice vinegar**
2 **teaspoons minced garlic**
1 **teaspoon Asian sesame oil**

2 **pounds boneless, skinless chicken breasts or thigh meat**
2 **red bell peppers**
6 **pearl onions**
Vegetable oil

To make the marinade, in a small bowl, whisk together the marinade ingredients.

Rinse the chicken under cold water and pat dry with paper towels. Cut into 1½-inch chunks. Remove the stems, ribs, and seeds from the bell peppers and cut into 1-inch chunks. Cut the pearl onions in half.

Place the chicken, bell peppers, and pearl onions in a large resealable plastic bag and pour in the marinade. Press the air out of the bag and seal tightly. Turn the bag to distribute the marinade, place in a bowl, and refrigerate for 30 minutes to 2 hours, turning occasionally.

Remove the chicken, bell peppers, and pearl onions from the bag and reserve the marinade. Pour the marinade into a small saucepan, bring to a boil, and boil for 1 full minute. Remove from the heat and set aside.

Thread the chicken, bell peppers, and pearl onions onto skewers. Lightly brush or spray with vegetable oil. Grill over direct medium heat until the meat is firm and the vegetables are tender, 8 to 10 minutes, turning and basting with the marinade once halfway through grilling time. Serve warm.

Savory Stuffed Tenderloin

Cheryl Jamison and Bill Jamison/Reprinted from *Born to Grill* (Harvard Common Press)

Serves 6 to 8

Most people enjoy fennel just for its savory, licorice taste, but it has other pluses as well. Romans believed fennel could control weight problems and people in medieval times believed it could ward off disease.

Fennel Rub
4 plump cloves garlic
1½ teaspoons fennel seed
1½ teaspoons kosher salt or other coarse salt
1 teaspoon whole black peppercorns
1 teaspoon crushed red pepper flakes

1 (2½-pound) beef tenderloin section, at least choice grade, with a pocket cut by your butcher

Spinach-Fennel Filling
1 tablespoon olive oil
1 small fennel bulb, cut into thin matchsticks
3 tablespoons minced red bell pepper
3 tablespoons minced onion
¼ pound fresh spinach, chopped

At least 2½ hours and up to 12 hours before you plan to grill the meat, prepare the spice rub. With a mortar and pestle or small food processor, combine the rub ingredients and purée the mixture. It will be grainy in texture. Coat the tenderloin thoroughly with the rub, massaging it inside and out. Wrap the meat in plastic and refrigerate.

Prepare the filling, first warming the oil in a medium skillet over medium heat. Add the fennel, bell pepper, and onion, and cook until softened, about 5 to 7 minutes. Stir in the spinach, cover the skillet, and reduce the heat. Cook for an additional 5 minutes or until the vegetables

are very tender. If any liquid remains, cook the filling for another 1 to 2 minutes, uncovered. The mixture should be moist but not wet. Set it aside to cool.

About 30 minutes before you plan to grill the tenderloin, remove it from the refrigerator and stuff it with the filling. Let it sit, covered, at room temperature.

Fire up the grill for a two-level fire capable of cooking first on high heat (1 to 2 seconds with the hand test) and then on medium heat (4 to 5 seconds with the hand test).

Grill the tenderloin, uncovered, over high heat for 4 to 5 minutes, rolling it frequently to sear all sides. Move the tenderloin to medium heat and continue grilling for 9 to 11 minutes for medium-rare doneness, again rolling on all sides. If grilling covered, sear the meat first on high heat, uncovered, for 4 to 5 minutes, rolling it frequently to sear all sides; finish cooking with the cover on over medium heat for 7 to 10 minutes, turning the tenderloin once midway.

Serve the tenderloin hot, sliced into thick medallions.

Madras-Style Meatball Kebabs

Jamie Purviance and Sandra S. McRae/Reprinted from *Weber's Big Book of Grilling* (Chronicle Books)

Serves 6 to 8

Curry powder, a blend of numerous spices—usually ground cumin, coriander, cinnamon, turmeric, black pepper, and chiles—comes in many different varieties. Madras curry powder is hotter than the regular varieties.

Sauce
2 tablespoons vegetable oil
1 cup finely chopped yellow onion
1 tablespoon minced garlic
1 tablespoon Madras-style curry powder
1 teaspoon ground cumin
1 tablespoon grated fresh ginger
1 (28-ounce) can plum tomatoes with juices
1 tablespoon firmly packed light brown sugar
1 teaspoon kosher salt
1/4 teaspoon freshly ground black pepper

Meatballs
6 tablespoons fine dry bread crumbs
2 large eggs
2 pounds ground lamb
2 tablespoons minced jalapeño pepper
2 teaspoons kosher salt
1/2 teaspoon freshly ground black pepper

2 large green bell peppers, quartered, stemmed, and seeded, cut into 1-inch pieces

Vegetable oil

To make the sauce, in a medium sauté pan over medium heat, warm the vegetable oil. Add the onion and cook, stirring occasionally, until golden, about 5 minutes. Add the garlic and cook 1 minute more. Stir in the curry powder and cumin. Cook for 30 seconds more. Stir in the ginger.

Remove the pan from the heat. Remove half of the mixture from the pan and reserve it to blend with the lamb.

In a food processor, purée the tomatoes and add to the onion mixture in the sauté pan. Add the brown sugar, salt, and pepper and bring to a boil over high heat. Reduce heat to a simmer and cook, stirring frequently, until the sauce is very thick and has reduced to about 1 1/2 cups, about 30 minutes. Set aside.

Meanwhile, make the meatballs. In a large bowl, combine the bread crumbs with 1/2 cup cold water. Allow to stand for about 5 minutes. Stir in the eggs. Add the lamb, jalapeño, salt, black pepper, and the reserved onion mixture. Gently stir with your fingers just until blended. Wet your hands with cold water and shape the meat into 40 balls, about 1 1/2 inches in diameter each. Be careful not to overwork the meat. Cover with plastic wrap and refrigerate for about 45 minutes or until very cold.

Thread the cold meatballs onto 8 skewers, 5 per skewer, alternating with the bell pepper. Lightly brush the meatballs and bell pepper with the vegetable oil. Grill over direct high heat until the meat is cooked to the center, 6 to 8 minutes, turning once halfway through grilling time. Meanwhile, reheat the sauce. Serve the kebabs hot with the sauce.

Swordfish Kebabs with Pasta Provençal

Jamie Purviance and Sandra S. McRae/Reprinted from *Weber's Big Book of Grilling* (Chronicle Books)

Serves 4

Served with a light salad, here's a quick, simple, and healthy meal. Marinate the fish in the morning and the whole dish comes together in no time.

Marinade
6 tablespoons extra virgin olive oil
¼ cup fresh lemon juice
2 teaspoons minced garlic
½ teaspoon crushed red pepper flakes
½ teaspoon kosher salt

2 pounds swordfish
1 small red onion

Pasta Provençal
¼ cup extra virgin olive oil
¼ cup finely diced yellow onion
1 tablespoon minced garlic
½ teaspoon crushed red pepper flakes
¼ cup dry white wine
2 cups coarsely chopped tomatoes
8 ounces angel hair pasta
¼ cup finely chopped fresh basil
Kosher salt
Freshly ground black pepper

To make the marinade, in a small bowl whisk together the marinade ingredients.

Cut the swordfish into 1-inch cubes. Quarter the onion and separate it into leaves. Place the fish and onion in a large resealable plastic bag and pour in the marinade. Press the air out of the bag and seal tightly. Turn the bag to distribute the marinade, place in a bowl, and refrigerate for 30 minutes.

To make the pasta, in a large sauté pan over medium-high heat, warm the oil and cook the onion until translucent, 2 to 3 minutes. Add the garlic and pepper flakes and cook for 1 to 2 minutes more. Add the wine and tomatoes; bring to a boil, then reduce the heat to a simmer. Keep warm over low heat.

In a large pot of boiling salted water, cook the pasta according to package directions until al dente. Drain and pour into the sauté pan. Toss to combine. Add the basil and season with salt and pepper. Set aside over very low heat.

Prepare a gas or charcoal grill.

Remove the swordfish and onion from the bag and discard the marinade. Thread the pieces alternately onto skewers. Grill over direct medium heat until the swordfish is cooked through but still moist, 6 to 8 minutes, turning once halfway through grilling time. Remove from the grill and serve warm with the pasta.

Chapter 5

DESSERTS

Sweet Cheese Puffs

Flo Braker/Reprinted from *Sweet Miniatures* (Chronicle Books)

Makes 2½ to 3 dozen 1½-inch puffs

This is one of the personal favorites of master baker Flo Braker, who tucks a dollop of lemon-and-vanilla-flavored cream cheese inside a rich, sour-cream pastry. Try embellishing the cheese filling by adding ½ cup of diced poached apple or pear pieces.

Sour Cream Pastry
2 cups unsifted all-purpose flour
⅛ teaspoon salt
1 cup (2 sticks) unsalted butter, chilled and cut into ¼-inch slices
½ cup sour cream

Cream Cheese Filling
8 ounces cream cheese
1 large egg
½ cup granulated sugar
1 teaspoon pure vanilla extract
1 teaspoon finely grated lemon zest

½ cup unsifted confectioners' sugar

Put the flour and salt in a 3-quart bowl; stir to blend. Scatter butter slices over the flour, and cut in with a pastry blender until the mixture consists of particles that vary in size from small peas to bread crumbs.

Stir in the sour cream with a fork. The pastry will appear dry, because the sour cream is thick and doesn't disperse easily. With your hands, manipulate the dough into a ball.

Divide the dough in three equal pieces. Shape each into a 5-inch square about ⅝ inch thick. Wrap in plastic and refrigerate until cold and firm, at least 4 hours.

To make the filling, process all filling ingredients in a food processor until the mixture is smooth.

Remove one pastry square from the refrigerator. Set aside for 10 minutes before rolling it. On a floured surface, roll the pastry into a rectangle slightly less than ⅛ inch thick. With a ruler and a pastry wheel, trim the ragged edges; then measure and cut the pastry into 3-inch squares.

Lay the pastry squares across the top of ungreased 12-cup miniature muffin pans, each cup measuring 1⅞ inches across and ¾ inch deep, centering each square over 1 cup. Spoon 1 heaping teaspoon of filling on each square; then bring opposite corners to the center and press lightly to seal. This process will also ease the pastry into each cup. Refrigerate for at least 30 minutes. Roll and shape the remaining pastry squares in the same fashion.

Adjust the rack to the lower third of the oven; preheat oven to 375 degrees F.

Bake 2 to 3 pans at a time for about 20 to 25 minutes, or until pastries are light brown. Remove the pan from the oven to a wire rack for about 10 minutes. Remove pastries from the pan to a wire rack to cool completely.

To decorate, sprinkle with confectioners' sugar before serving at room temperature.

If not serving the same day baked, stack undecorated pastries in airtight sturdy plastic containers and freeze up to 2 weeks. To serve, reheat to freshen in a 325 degree F oven for about 7 to 12 minutes, or until warm; cool slightly, then sprinkle with the confectioners' sugar.

Note: If you feel like embellishing the cheese filling a bit, it's nice to add ½ cup diced poached apple or pear pieces. In the fall, I suggest you look for quinces in the produce section of the supermarket. Add ½ cup poached and diced quince to the cream cheese filling. Though it is a richly flavored fruit, it is not as popular as the apple or pear. In my opinion, seeing the quince's golden peach color, inhaling its distinct scent, and tasting its concentrated perfume is culinary magnificence.

Chocolate Cherry Chaps

Flo Braker/Reprinted from *Sweet Miniatures* (Chronicle Books)

Makes 8 dozen 1½-inch round fluted tartlets

*Here's a tempting treat for people who understand the passionate connection
between cherries and chocolate. A single cherry dipped in creamy, dark chocolate
glaze sits inside a cherry-glazed tartlet.*

Pastry
2½ cups unsifted all-purpose flour
⅛ teaspoon salt
⅓ cup granulated sugar
1 cup (2 sticks) unsalted butter, chilled and cut
   into ¼-inch slices
1 large egg
1 teaspoon pure vanilla extract

Filling
2 cups sour cherry jelly

Dark Chocolate Fruit Glaze
1 cup (2 sticks) unsalted butter
10 ounces semisweet chocolate, finely chopped
2 ounces unsweetened chocolate, finely chopped
8 dozen (2 pounds) fresh bing cherries with
   stems, at room temperature

To make the pastry, put the flour, salt, and sugar
in a food processor bowl. Process just to blend
ingredients. Scatter all the butter slices over the
flour mixture, and process with on/off bursts
until the mixture has the consistency of cornmeal.

Whisk the egg and vanilla together in a small
bowl. With the motor on, pour the egg mixture
down the feed tube. Process until the ingredients form a ball. Remove the dough to a work
surface, and with the heel of your hand, press
dough together until it is smooth and cohesive.

Adjust rack to the lower third of the oven and
preheat oven to 350 degrees F. Arrange 4 dozen
ungreased 1½-inch fluted tartlet tins close
together on a 12 by 15½ by ½-inch baking sheet.

Pinch off 1 teaspoon of dough and drop it into a
tin. Repeat until all tins contain dough. One by
one, roll each piece of dough into a ball in the
palm of your hands. This step aids in shaping
the tartlet shells more evenly. To press the dough
into tins, with index finger, press the center of
dough ball into the tin, then press the dough up
the sides while rotating the tin to distribute the
dough evenly. The object is to use just enough
dough to line the tartlet tin without creating a
thick shell. (Notice that I recommend complet-
ing one task before beginning another: Fill the
baking sheet with tins, pinch off a teaspoon of
dough for each tin, roll dough between your

palms to form a smooth ball, and last press the balls evenly into the tins. Handling one movement at a time is easier and faster. You discover your own rhythm from the repetition.)

Bake tartlet shells for 12 to 15 minutes, or until light golden. Remove baking sheet from oven to rack to cool. When the tins are cool enough to touch, squeeze each tin gently with your thumb and forefinger, turn it upside down, and let the miniature tartlet shell drop into the palm of your hand.

Repeat the filling and baking procedure with the remaining dough.

Arrange the baked, cooled tartlet shells on a large tray or baking sheet. (Cooled shells may be stacked in an airtight metal container and stored at room temperature for up to 1 week.)

To make the filling, heat the jelly in a small saucepan just to warm and liquefy it. Using a pastry brush, coat each shell with a thin glaze of jelly.

To make the glaze, place the butter and chocolates in a 2-quart bowl that fits snugly over a saucepan half filled with 120 degree to 130 degree F water, to melt ingredients. Stir occasionally until smooth. If necessary, maintain the water's temperature over very low heat.

Dip the cherries, one at a time, into the liquid chocolate glaze, and then set each cherry in a tartlet shell. With scissors, trim each cherry stem, leaving a stem between ½ inch and ¾ inch. (Clipping the stems decorates each tartlet uniformly and reminds the person eating it that the cherry contains a pit.)

Store tartlets in 1 layer in a covered foil-lined cardboard container, such as a cake box, at room temperature up to 1 day.

Harlequins

Flo Braker/Reprinted from *Sweet Miniatures* (Chronicle Books)

Makes 4 dozen 1½-inch cookies

This simple—but delicious—cookie, scented with orange and lemon zest, transforms into an elegant dessert with the use of two glazes made from apricot jam and red currant jelly.

Dough

1 cup (2 sticks) unsalted butter at room
   temperature
⅓ cup unsifted confectioners' sugar
⅓ cup granulated sugar
⅛ teaspoon salt
1 egg yolk
½ teaspoon each finely grated lemon and
   orange zest
½ teaspoon pure vanilla extract
2 cups unsifted all-purpose flour

Jelly Glaze

⅔ cup strained apricot jam
⅔ cup red currant jelly

Sugar Glaze

½ cup unsifted confectioners' sugar
4 teaspoons water
Additional confectioners' sugar

To make the dough, in a large bowl of a stand mixer, cream the butter at medium-low speed until it is smooth, about 1 minute. Beat in the sugars and salt at medium speed until creamy. Add the egg yolk, then the citrus zests and vanilla, mixing just until the mixture is well combined and slightly fluffy, scraping down the sides of the bowl. Lower mixer speed, and gradually add flour, mixing only until mixture is thoroughly combined.

Divide the dough in thirds, roll out each portion of dough between 2 sheets of waxed paper to form a circle 10 inches in diameter and ⅛ inch thick. Leaving the dough circles between waxed paper, stack them on a baking sheet and refrigerate until firm, for at least 2 hours or up to 3 days; or freeze, well wrapped, up to 1 month.

Adjust rack to lower third of oven and preheat to 325 degrees F. Line 2 large cool baking sheets with parchment paper.

Remove 1 dough package at a time from the refrigerator. Peel off top waxed paper sheet, replace it loosely on top, and flip the entire package over. Peel off and discard the second sheet of waxed paper.

Using a 1½-inch cutter of any shape, cut out shapes in the dough and set them ½ inch apart on the baking sheets. Bake, 1 sheet at a time, for

12 to 15 minutes, or until the cookies are no longer shiny, just ivory colored, and feel slightly firm (lightly touch a few). Place the baking sheets on a wire rack until the cookies are cool.

To make the jelly glaze, keep the oven rack in the same position; lower the oven temperature to 140 degrees F. Place the apricot jam and currant jelly in two small saucepans. Simmer on low heat for 2 minutes to evaporate some liquid before decorating the cookies. Cool just until warm.

Brush warm apricot jam over half of one cookie's surface. With a clean brush, paint the other half with the currant jelly. Paint the remaining cookies, setting them as you finish about ¼ inch apart on 1 large clean baking sheet.

To make the sugar glaze, mix the sugar and water together until smooth. With a clean pastry brush, paint a thin coating of glaze over the jelly-glazed cookies. The glaze's consistency should be thin enough that a transparent film covers the jellies. Adjust the consistency by adding 1 teaspoon water at a time if it is too thick or more sugar if it is too thin. Place cookies in the preheated oven until the glaze is set and dry, about 10 minutes. Place the baking sheet on a wire rack to cool for 5 minutes; then, lift the cookies from the baking sheet with a metal spatula to a rack to cool.

Stack undecorated cookies in an airtight metal container and store at room temperature up to 10 days. Store decorated cookies in 1 layer in a covered foil-lined cardboard container, such as a cake box, at room temperature for up to 3 days.

Coconut Rice Pudding with Tropical Nuts

Rick Rodgers/Reprinted from *On Rice* (Chronicle Books)

Serves 6 to 8

Coconut milk turns ordinary rice pudding into a very special, rich treat.
Be careful not to purchase cream of coconut, which is too sweet for this dish.

2 cups cooked medium-grain rice
3 cups canned unsweetened coconut milk
¾ cup plus 2 tablespoons packed light
   brown sugar
4 large egg yolks
2 tablespoons cornstarch
1 teaspoon vanilla
2 cups chopped ripe fruits, such as mango,
   papaya, banana, and raspberries, in any
   combination
Sweetened whipped cream, for garnish

In a heavy-bottomed, medium saucepan, bring the rice and coconut milk to a simmer over medium heat. Reduce the heat to low and cook, stirring often, until the rice is very soft, about 10 minutes. Stir in the brown sugar until dissolved.

In a medium bowl, whisk the egg yolks and cornstarch. Gradually whisk in about ½ cup of the hot rice mixture. Pour into the saucepan and cook, stirring constantly, until it comes to a simmer, then stir for 1 minute. Stir in the vanilla. Transfer to a medium bowl. Press a piece of plastic wrap directly onto the surface of the pudding. Using a small sharp knife, poke a few holes to act as vents in the plastic wrap. Cool the pudding to room temperature. Refrigerate until chilled, at least 4 hours or overnight.

Spoon the rice pudding into large wine glasses, layering with the fruit. Top with a dollop of whipped cream and serve immediately.

Gingered Coconut Rice Pudding Variation
Stir ½ cup finely chopped crystallized ginger into the pudding with the vanilla. Garnish each serving with additional chopped crystallized ginger.

Coconut Macaroons

David Lebovitz/Reprinted from *Room for Dessert* (HarperCollins Publishers)

Makes about 60 cookies

Ethereal is the only word that aptly describes these macaroons from master baker David Lebovitz. Each bite brings a sweet crunch and creaminess followed by a wave of chocolate. Truly delicious.

8 egg whites
2½ cups sugar
½ teaspoon salt
2 tablespoons honey
5 cups unsweetened dried coconut
½ cup flour
1 teaspoon vanilla extract
4 ounces bittersweet chocolate, chopped

Position 2 oven racks in the center and upper part of the oven. Preheat the oven to 350 degrees F.

In a large pan with a heavy bottom, warm the egg whites, sugar, salt, and honey, stirring over medium heat.

When the egg whites are warm to the touch, stir in the coconut, flour, and vanilla. Continue cooking over medium heat, stirring constantly, until the mixture is slightly dry and the bottom has just begun to sizzle and scorch. Cool. (You can refrigerate the mixture at this point for up to a week.)

When cool enough to handle, form the mixture into 1½-inch mounds with your fingers and space them evenly on parchment-lined baking sheets. Bake for 18 to 20 minutes, rotating the baking sheets and switching racks midway through baking so the macaroons brown evenly. Cool.

Cover a baking sheet with plastic wrap. Melt the chocolate in a clean, dry bowl set over barely simmering water. When the chocolate is almost completely melted, remove the bowl from the heat and stir until the chocolate is fully melted. Holding each cookie by the top, dip the bottom in the melted chocolate, removing any excess chocolate by scraping the bottom against the inside rim of the chocolate bowl. Set the cookies on the plastic-lined baking sheet with the chocolate side down. Refrigerate until the chocolate has hardened, and serve.

Champagne Gelée with Citrus Fruits and Kumquats

David Lebovitz/Reprinted from *Room for Dessert* (HarperCollins Publishers)

Serves 6

Your guests will appreciate the light and delicate qualities of this dessert, which will leave them feeling satisfied, but not overstuffed. If you choose to use a gold leaf or varak for added decoration, it can be purchased in Indian food stores or specialty baking supply stores.

Champagne Gelée
1 cup water
2 envelopes powdered gelatin
1 cup sugar
1 (750 ml) good-quality champagne, Prosecco, or Asti sparkling wine
Juice of ½ lime

2 tablespoons sugar
½ cup water
12 kumquats, rinsed
3 pink grapefruits
4 navel or blood oranges
Soft candied citrus peel
Gold leaf (optional)

To make the gelée, pour ½ cup of the water into a large bowl. Sprinkle the gelatin over the water and allow it to soften for 5 minutes.

Heat the remaining ½ cup of the water with the sugar until the sugar is dissolved.

After the gelatin has soaked for 5 minutes, pour the hot sugar water over the gelatin and stir until the gelatin granules have completely dissolved. Add the champagne, which will foam up (the reason for the large bowl I told you to use!), and lime juice. Test and add more lime juice if desired.

Cover the champagne mixture and refrigerate until set, at least 6 hours. To speed the jelling, first stir the gelée in an ice bath until it begins to thicken.

Heat the 2 tablespoons sugar and the ½ cup water until the sugar is dissolved. While the mixture is heating, slice the kumquats, discarding the end pieces and the seeds. Add the kumquats to the syrup and allow them to soak for 15 minutes, then drain off the syrup.

Peel and remove the sections and membranes from both the grapefruits and the oranges. Discard any seeds.

Choose 6 attractive stemmed glasses. Spoon some of the chilled gelée into each glass. Add a few sections of the fruits, some strips of candied peel, and a few pieces of gold leaf, if using. Spoon more of the gelée over the fruit. Continue to layer fruits and gelée with the gold leaf and candied peel until each glass is finished. Chill until ready to serve.

Table setting by Villeroy & Boch.

Strawberry Pineapple Pie

Wilfred Beriau, CEC, AAC, CCE/ Reprinted from *American Harvest* (Lebhar-Friedman Books)

Serves 6 to 8

This pie is quick and easy to make; the combination of strawberries and pineapple covered with a sprinkling of coconut is a real treat.

Pie Shell
1⅓ cups all-purpose flour
1 teaspoon sugar
¼ teaspoon salt
⅛ teaspoon baking powder
½ cup (1 stick) unsalted butter, cold, cut into small cubes
2 to 3 tablespoons ice water

Filling
2 cups diced fresh pineapple
3 cups diced fresh strawberries
1⅓ cups sugar
¼ cup cornstarch
½ cup all-purpose flour
⅓ cup cold unsalted butter, cut into pieces
⅓ cup packaged sweetened coconut

Whipped cream or ice cream

To prepare the pie shell, in a food processor with the fitted metal blade, process the flour, sugar, salt, and baking powder to combine, 5 seconds. Add the butter cubes to the flour and process for about 15 seconds, or until the mixture resembles coarse meal.

Add no more than 2 tablespoons ice water and pulse a few times. Pinch a small amount of the mixture between your fingers. If it does not hold together, add the remaining tablespoon of water and pulse again. The mixture should be crumbly and will not hold together without being pinched. Using your hands, gather the dough together in a ball. Wrap with plastic wrap, flatten it into a disk, and refrigerate for at least 30 minutes, preferably overnight.

Preheat the oven to 350 degrees F.

To roll, unwrap the dough and place it on a lightly flour-dusted flat surface. Roll the dough, pressing lightly, from the center out, dusting with flour, as necessary, on and under the dough to prevent sticking. Continue to roll until it is at least 10 inches in diameter and less than ¼ inch thick.

Center the dough in a 9-inch pie plate. Press the dough to the bottom and around the sides. Trim, leaving ¼- to ½-inch reserve all the way around. Crimp the dough between two fingers to form a decorative crust. Place a piece of foil wrap on the bottom of the dough and fill with dried beans or pie weights. Prebake the crust, 10 to 12 minutes. Set aside to cool on a wire rack.

To make the filling, in a large bowl, combine the pineapple, strawberries, 1 cup of the sugar, and the cornstarch. Stir to combine, then transfer the mixture to the prebaked pie crust.

In a small bowl, mix the flour with the remaining ⅓ cup sugar. Using two knives, cut the butter pieces into the flour. Evenly distribute this crumb topping over the fruit; sprinkle with coconut. Bake 35 minutes. Serve slightly warm with a dollop of whipped cream or ice cream.

Strawberries Balsamico

Jamie Purviance and Sandra S. McRae/Reprinted from *Weber's Big Book of Grilling* (Chronicle Books)

Serves 8

Here's an unforgettable berry sauce to serve with vanilla ice cream and fresh strawberries.
Strawberries are marinated in a balsamic-orange mixture, then grilled and puréed.
Try to purchase strawberries that are red all the way to the stem.

2 pounds fresh strawberries, hulled

¼ cup granulated sugar
¼ cup balsamic vinegar
1 teaspoon grated orange zest
1 teaspoon orange-flavored liqueur (optional)
8 scoops vanilla ice cream

Place half of the strawberries in a medium bowl.

In a small bowl, whisk together the sugar, vinegar, orange zest, and liqueur. Pour the liquid over the strawberries in the bowl, turning them to coat evenly. Allow to stand for 15 minutes. Strain, reserving the liquid.

Thread the coated strawberries onto skewers. Grill over direct medium heat until lightly marked, 4 to 5 minutes, turning once halfway through grilling time. Allow to cool slightly. Purée the grilled strawberries along with the reserved liquid in a food processor.

Slice the remaining strawberries. Add the purée to the sliced berries. Pour the strawberry mixture over the ice cream and serve.

Fresh Ginger Cake

David Lebovitz/Reprinted from *Room for Dessert* (HarperCollins Publishers)

Makes one 9- or 9½-inch cake (serves 10 to 12)

*Using fresh ginger, David Lebovitz, a well-known pastry chef in San Francisco, created this
bold and memorable cake, which stays moist for days. It has become so popular in San Francisco
that it appears on a number of restaurant menus as "David's Ginger Cake."*

**4 ounces fresh ginger
1 cup mild molasses
1 cup sugar
1 cup vegetable oil, preferably peanut
2½ cups flour
1 teaspoon ground cinnamon
½ teaspoon ground cloves
½ teaspoon ground black pepper
1 cup water
2 teaspoons baking soda
2 eggs, at room temperature**

Position the oven rack in the center of the oven.
Preheat the oven to 350 degrees F. Line a 9 by 3-
inch round cake pan or a 9½-inch springform
pan with a circle of parchment paper.

Peel, slice, and chop the ginger very fine with a
knife (or use a grater).

Mix together the molasses, sugar, and oil. In
another bowl, sift together the flour, cinnamon,
cloves, and black pepper.

Bring the water to a boil in a saucepan, stir in
the baking soda, and then mix the hot water
into the molasses mixture. Stir in the ginger.

Gradually whisk the dry ingredients into the
batter. Add the eggs, and continue mixing until
everything is thoroughly combined. Pour the
batter into the prepared cake pan and bake for
about 1 hour, until the top of the cake springs
back lightly when pressed or a toothpick inserted
into the center comes out clean. If the top of the
cake browns too quickly before the cake is done,
drape a piece of foil over it and continue baking.

Cool the cake for at least 30 minutes. Run a
knife around the edge of the cake to loosen it
from the pan. Remove the cake from the pan and
peel off the parchment paper.

Citrus Pound Cake

Marvin Woods/Reprinted from *The New Low-Country Cooking* (William Morrow & Co.)

Serves 8 to 10

Pound cake got its name because it was traditionally made with a pound each of flour, sugar, butter, and eggs and boosted with a shot of vanilla. This flavorful cake uses citrus flavorings for an even more delicious result.

¾ cup (1½ sticks) unsalted butter, softened
¾ cup granulated sugar
Juice of 1 orange
Juice of 1 lemon
Juice of 1 lime
1½ teaspoons vanilla extract
3 large eggs
2¾ cups all-purpose flour
1½ teaspoons baking powder
Pinch of salt
Confectioners' sugar, for dusting (optional)

Preheat the oven to 350 degrees F. Butter a 9-inch-diameter Bundt pan.

In a large bowl, using an stand mixer set on medium speed, cream together the butter and sugar until the mixture is light and fluffy, about 5 minutes. Beat in the 3 juices and the vanilla. One at a time, beat in the eggs, beating well after each addition.

In another mixing bowl, sift together the flour, baking powder, and salt. Stir the flour mixture into the batter until combined. Scrape the mixture into the prepared pan and bake for 40 to 45 minutes, or until a toothpick inserted in the center of the cake comes out clean. Transfer the Bundt pan to a wire rack and let cool for 10 minutes. Then turn the cake out of the pan and let it cool completely on the rack. Dust the top with confectioners' sugar, if desired, just before serving.

Chocolate Cupcake Cones

Abigail Johnson Dodge/Reprinted from Williams-Sonoma's The Kid's Cookbook (Time-Life Books)

Makes 10 cupcakes

Here's an ingenious recipe from Williams-Sonoma's cookbook for children in which a moist chocolate cake is cooked inside cupcake cones.

10 flat-bottomed waffle cones
1 cup all-purpose flour
⅓ cup unsweetened cocoa powder
1¾ teaspoons baking powder
¼ teaspoon salt
¼ cup (½ stick) butter, at room temperature, cut into pieces
½ cup sugar
1 egg
½ cup milk
1 teaspoon vanilla extract
1 recipe Creamy Frosting (recipe follows)
Colored sprinkles

Preheat the oven to 350 degrees F. Check the cones for holes or cracks and replace if necessary. Put each cone into a cup of a muffin pan.

In a small mixing bowl, combine the flour, cocoa, baking powder, and salt. Stir with a table fork until blended.

In a medium mixing bowl, combine the butter, sugar, and egg. Using an stand mixer set on medium speed, beat until the mixture is lighter in color and no lumps remain, about 2 minutes. Turn off the mixer a few times so you can scrape down the sides of the bowl with a rubber spatula.

Add the milk and vanilla. Reduce the speed to low and beat until smooth, stopping to scrape down the sides of the bowl as needed. Add the flour mixture to the butter-sugar mixture all at once. Using the rubber spatula, stir gently until the batter is completely moistened and combined.

Using a spoon, place even amounts of the batter, about 3 tablespoons, into each cone. Gently tap the bottom of the cone on your palm to settle the batter.

Bake the cupcakes until a toothpick inserted in the center of 1 cake comes out clean, 25 to 28 minutes. Using oven mitts, remove the muffin pan from the oven and set it on a wire rack. Let cool completely.

Using an icing spatula, spread 1 heaping table-spoon of the frosting on each cupcake. Using your fingers, sprinkle the tops with the colored sprinkles. Serve immediately or cover loosely with plastic wrap and store at room temperature for up to 1 day.

Creamy Frosting
Makes 1 cup

6 tablespoons (¾ stick) butter, at room temperature
1½ cups confectioners' sugar, sifted if lumpy
2 tablespoons heavy cream
¾ teaspoon vanilla extract
Food coloring (optional)
3 ounces unsweetened chocolate, chopped
    (optional)

To make vanilla frosting, in a medium mixing bowl, combine the butter, confectioners' sugar, cream, and vanilla. Using an stand mixer set on low speed, beat until the mixture is smooth. Turn off the mixer several times so you can scrape down the sides of the bowl with a rubber spatula. Use the frosting immediately.

To make colored frosting, make the frosting as directed. Add a drop or two of food coloring to the frosting and mix until thoroughly blended. Alternatively, divide the frosting among 2 or 3 small bowls and mix a different color into each bowl. Use the frosting immediately.

To make chocolate frosting, make the frosting as directed. Fill a small saucepan half full with water. Choose a small, deep heatproof bowl that fits snugly on the saucepan. Be sure the bottom of the bowl does not touch the water. Add the chocolate to the small bowl and set the whole thing (water-filled pan and bowl) over medium heat. Heat the chocolate, stirring with a wooden spoon, until it is melted, about 5 minutes. Using a potholder, remove the pan from the heat. Ask an adult to help you remove the bowl from the saucepan of water. Be careful: The steam is very hot! Set the bowl aside to cool. Stir the melted and cooled chocolate into the frosting until well blended. Use the frosting immediately.

Dahlia Pear Tart with Caramel Sauce

Tom Douglas/Reprinted from *Tom Douglas' Seattle Kitchen* (William Morrow & Co.)

Serves 6

Another signature recipe from star Seattle chef Tom Douglas, it makes a beautiful presentation to impress your guests. This tart's rich caramel sauce, crisp pastry, and vanilla-scented pears are irresistible. To save time, use a commercial high-quality caramel sauce.

Poached Pears
3 (7-ounce) pears, ripe but firm, such as Bartlett
  or Bosc
4 cups water
2 cups sugar
1 vanilla bean, sliced in half lengthwise

Almond Cream
3 tablespoons almond paste
2 tablespoons sugar
1½ tablespoons unsalted butter, softened
1 large egg yolk

About 1 pound store-bought frozen puff pastry
Caramel Sauce (recipe follows)
Whipped cream

To poach the pears, peel and cut them in half lengthwise. Trim out the stem and blossom end and remove the core with a melon baller or paring knife. Combine the water and sugar in a large saucepan. Scrape the seeds from the vanilla bean and add the seeds, pod, and pears to the pan. To keep the pears submerged while they poach, put a sheet of parchment paper on the surface and weight it with a plate or small lid. Place the saucepan over high heat. When the liquid comes to a boil, turn the heat down to a simmer. The amount of time it will take to poach the pears depends on their ripeness, probably 15 to 20 minutes after the pears come to a simmer. Test for doneness by poking a pear with a point of a small knife. As soon as the pears are tender but not mushy, remove the saucepan from the heat. Allow them to cool in the liquid.

To make the almond cream, cream the almond paste and sugar together in a small mixing bowl of an stand mixer or in a food processor. The mixture will look crumbly. Beat in the butter, bit by bit. Add the egg yolk and mix until creamy and smooth. Set aside.

On a lightly floured work surface, roll the puff pastry dough out into a 9 by 15-inch rectangle. Trim the dough with a knife to straighten the edges. The dough should be about ⅛ thick. Cut into 6 squares about 4½ inches on a side; that is, cut the 9-inch length of dough in half to make two 4½-inch strips, then cut the strips 3 times into squares. Place the squares on a parchment paper–lined baking sheet and set it in the freezer. Freeze the squares at least 10 to 15 minutes before assembling and baking.

Preheat the oven to 425 degrees F. Remove the pastry squares from the freezer and spread about 2 teaspoons of almond cream in the center of each pastry square. Remove the pears from the poaching liquid. (You can save the poaching liquid for poaching other fruit or discard.) Blot-dry the pears on a clean kitchen towel, then slice each pear half lengthwise in ¼-inch-thick slices. Lift each sliced pear half with a spatula and place it over the almond cream, fanning it gently.

Slip another baking sheet underneath to "double pan" and protect the bottoms of the tarts. Set the baking sheet in the oven and bake for 20 minutes, until the tarts are puffed and golden brown. Remove from the oven.

Ladle some warm Caramel Sauce on each plate. Using a spatula, transfer a warm pear tart to the plate. Garnish with a mound of whipped cream.

Note: The pears can be poached ahead and stored, covered with their poaching liquid, in the refrigerator for a few days. The almond cream can be made a few days ahead and stored, tightly covered, in the refrigerator. You can bake the pear tarts early in the day and leave them at room temperature. Reheat them in a preheated 375 degree F oven for about 5 minutes before serving.

Caramel Sauce
Makes 1½ cups

1⅓ cups sugar
⅓ cup water
1 cup heavy cream
2 tablespoons (¼ stick) unsalted butter, softened

Place the sugar and water in a heavy-bottomed saucepan over medium-low heat, whisking occasionally until the sugar is completely dissolved, about 3 minutes. After the sugar is dissolved, raise the heat to high and bring the mixture to a boil, without stirring, until the syrup turns a deep golden brown, 15 to 20 minutes.

If you see the sugar caramelizing only in one corner, you can gently tilt or rotate the pan to distribute the color evenly, but do not whisk. When the syrup has colored nicely, remove the pan from the heat and immediately add the heavy cream; be careful and stand back because the mixture will sputter. Do not stir until the mixture settles. Return the pan to low heat and stir with a wooden spoon until the strands of caramel melt. Remove from the heat and stir in the butter. Serve warm.

Note: This can be made ahead and stored, covered, in the refrigerator for a few days. Warm it over hot water in a double boiler before serving.

Triple Coconut Cream Pie

Tom Douglas/Reprinted from *Tom Douglas' Seattle Kitchen* (William Morrow & Co.)

Makes one 9-inch pie (serves 6 to 8)

This pie has been a best-seller at Tom Douglas's Seattle restaurants for over twelve years. It's a triple hit for coconut lovers who will find their beloved ingredient in the filling, crust, and topping.

Pastry Cream

2 cups milk

2 cups sweetened shredded coconut

1 vanilla bean, split in half lengthwise

2 large eggs

½ cup plus 2 tablespoons sugar

3 tablespoons all-purpose flour

¼ cup (½ stick) unsalted butter, softened

1 (9-inch) Coconut Pie Shell (recipe follows),
  prebaked and cooled

Topping

2½ cups heavy cream, chilled

⅓ cup sugar

1 teaspoon pure vanilla extract

2 ounces unsweetened "chip" or large-shred
  coconut (about 1½ cups) or sweetened shredded
  coconut, for garnish

4 to 6 ounces white chocolate chunks (to make
  2 ounces of curls)

Combine the milk and the coconut in a medium saucepan. Scrape the seeds from the vanilla bean and add both the seeds and the pod to the milk mixture. Place the saucepan over medium-high heat and stir occasionally until the mixture almost comes to a boil.

In a bowl, whisk together the eggs, sugar, and flour until well combined. Temper the eggs (to keep them from scrambling) by pouring a small amount (about ⅓ cup) of the scalded milk into the egg mixture while whisking. Then add the warmed egg mixture into the saucepan of milk and coconut. Whisk over medium-high heat until the pastry cream thickens and begins to bubble. Keep whisking until the mixture is very thick, 4 to 5 minutes more. Remove the saucepan from the heat. Add the butter and whisk until it melts. Remove and discard the vanilla pod. Transfer the pastry cream to a bowl and place it over a bowl of ice water. Stir occasionally until it is cool. Place a piece of plastic wrap directly on the surface of the pastry cream to prevent a crust from forming and refrigerate until completely cold. The pastry cream will thicken as it cools.

When the pastry cream is cold, fill the prebaked pie shell with it, smoothing the surface. In an stand mixer with the whisk, whip the heavy cream with the sugar and vanilla on medium speed. Gradually increase the speed to high and whip to peaks that are firm enough to hold their shape. Fill a pastry bag fitted with the star tip with the whipped cream and pipe it all over the surface of the pie, or spoon it over.

Preheat the oven to 350 degrees F. Spread the coconut chips on a baking sheet and toast in the oven, watching carefully and stirring once or twice since coconut burns easily, until lightly browned, 7 to 8 minutes. Use a vegetable peeler to scrape about 2 ounces of the white chocolate into curls.

Cut the pie into 6 to 8 wedges and place on dessert plates. Decorate each wedge with the white chocolate curls and the toasted coconut.

Note: If not serving immediately, keep the pie refrigerated, covered with plastic wrap. The finished pie should be consumed within a day. Prepare the garnishes just before serving. The coconut pastry cream can be made a day ahead and stored chilled in the refrigerator, covered with plastic wrap as described. Fill the pie shell and top it with whipped cream and garnishes when you are ready to serve the pie.

Coconut Pie Shell
Makes one 9-inch shell

1 cup plus 2 tablespoons all-purpose flour
½ cup sweetened shredded coconut
½ cup (1 stick) cold unsalted butter, cut into ½-inch dice
2 teaspoons sugar
¼ teaspoon kosher salt
⅓ cup ice water, or more as needed

In a food processor, combine the flour, coconut, diced butter, sugar, and salt. Pulse to form coarse crumbs. Gradually add the water, a tablespoon at a time, pulsing each time. Use only as much water as needed for the dough to hold together when gently pressed between your fingers; don't work the dough with your hands, just test it to see if it is holding. The dough will not form a ball or even clump together in the food processor—it will still be quite loose.

Place a large sheet of plastic wrap on the counter and dump the coconut dough onto it. Pull the plastic wrap around the dough, forcing it into a rough flattened round with the pressure of the plastic wrap. Chill for 30 minutes to 1 hour before rolling.

To roll the dough, unwrap the round coconut dough and put it on a lightly floured work board. Flour the rolling pin and your hands. Roll the dough out into a circle about ⅛ inch thick. Lift the dough with a board scraper occasionally to check that it is not sticking and add more flour if it seems to stick. Trim to a 12- to 13-inch circle.

Transfer the rolled dough to a 9-inch pie pan. Ease the dough loosely and gently into the pan. You don't want to stretch the dough at this point because it will shrink when it is baked. Trim any excess dough to a 1- to 1 ½-inch overhang. Turn the dough under along the rim of the pie pan and use your finger to flute the edge. Chill the unbaked pie shell at least 1 hour before baking. This step prevents the dough from shrinking in the oven.

When you are ready to bake the piecrust, preheat the oven to 400 degrees F. Place a sheet of aluminum foil or parchment paper in the pie shell and fill with dried beans. Bake the piecrust until the pastry is golden, 20 to 25 minutes. Remove the pie pan from the oven. Remove the foil and beans and return the piecrust to the oven. Bake until the bottom of the crust has golden brown patches, 10 to 12 minutes. Remove from the oven and allow to cool before filling.

Note: The dough can be wrapped in plastic wrap and stored in the refrigerator for a day or two, or frozen for a few weeks. Also, the dough can be rolled out and fitted into a pie pan, and the unbaked pie shell can be wrapped in plastic wrap and refrigerated or frozen for the same amounts of time. Frozen pie shells can be baked directly out of the freezer, without thawing; the baking times will be a bit longer.

INDEX

Permissions

From *On Rice: 60 Fast and Easy Toppings That Make a Meal* by Rick Rodgers (Chronicle Books, 1997) © 1997 by Rick Rodgers: Chicken Breasts in Jambalaya Sauce, Korean Beef on Fiery Chinese Cabbage, and Coconut Rice Pudding with Tropical Nuts.

From *Simply Shrimp: 101 Recipes for Everybody's Favorite Seafood* by Rick Rodgers (Chronicle Books, 1998) © 1998 by Rick Rodgers: Moroccan-Spiced Shrimp on Fruited Couscous, Buttermilk Biscuits with Low Country Shrimp and Ham, Shrimp Stock, and Coconut Shrimp with Easy Peanut Sauce.

From *American Harvest: Recipes from Fifty of America's Premier Chefs* by the American Academy of Chefs, edited by Fritz Sonnenschmidt (Lebhar-Friedman Books, 2000) © 2000 by the American Academy of Chefs: Jersey Shore Grilled Chicken, Tomato, and Crab; Salad of Frisée and Tangerine with Grilled Sweet Potato; and Strawberry Pineapple Pie.

From *The Sticks and Stones Cookbook* by Ted Reader and Kathleen Sloan (Macmillan Canada, 1999) © 1999 by Ted Reader and Kathleen Sloan: Pine Needle–Smoked Mussels, Cedar-Planked Salmon Fillets with Shallot and Dill Crust, Bone Dust Barbecue Spice, Maple-Planked Brie with Roasted Garlic and Peppers, and Plank-Roasted Root Vegetables.

From *Bruce Aidells' Complete Sausage Book: Recipes from America's Premier Sausage Maker* by Bruce Aidells with Denis Kelly (Ten Speed Press, 2000) © 2000 by Bruce Aidells and Denis Kelly: Italian Turkey and Sundried Tomato Sausage and Penne with Roasted Tomatoes, Eggplant, and Italian Turkey Sausage.

From *The Complete Meat Cookbook* by Bruce Aidells and Denis Kelly (Houghton Mifflin Company, 1998) © 1998 by Bruce Aidells and Denis Kelly: Sautéed Pork Chops with Wilted Greens, Pine Nuts, and Raisins.

From Robert Clark: Grilled Mongolian Lamb with Stir-Fried Vegetables, Smoked Sablefish and Oyster Stew, and Dungeness Crab and Celery Root Salad.

From *Born to Grill: An American Celebration* by Cheryl Alter Jamison and Bill Jamison (Harvard Common Press, 1998) © 1998 by Cheryl Alter Jamison and Bill Jamison: Scallop and Melon Kebabs, Peach Vinegar, Glazed Mushroom Pasta, Wilted Fancy Lettuces, and Savory Stuffed Tenderloin.

From *Room for Dessert* by David Lebovitz (HarperCollins Publishers, 1999) © 1999 by David Lebovitz: Coconut Macaroons, Champagne Gelée with Citrus Fruits and Kumquats, and Fresh Ginger Cake.

From *Elegant Irish Cooking* by Noel C. Cullen (Lebhar-Friedman Books, 2001) © 2001 by Noel Cullen: Carrots in Orange Sauce, Cream of Watercress Soup with Herbal Drop Scones, and Honey-Glazed Breast of Duck with Peppercorn Dressing on a Bed of Spiced Celeriac.

From *The New Low-Country Cooking: 125 Recipes for Coastal Southern Cooking with Innovative Style* by Marvin Woods (William Morrow & Co., 2000) © 2000 by Marvin Woods: Creole Braised Chicken with Golden Rice, Creole Sauce, Vegetable Gumbo, Marv's Bay Spice, and Citrus Pound Cake.

From *Cracking the Coconut: Classic Thai Home Cooking* by Su-Mei Yu (William Morrow & Co., 2000) © 2000 by Su-Mei Yu: Miang Khum ("Savory Bite"), Padd Thai Bann Gog ("Bangkok-Style Padd Thai"), and Roasted Dried Chile Powder.

From Williams-Sonoma's *The Kid's Cookbook: A Great Book for Kids Who Love to Cook,* General Editor Chuck Williams (Time-Life Books, 2000) © 2000 by Weldon Owen, Inc. and Williams-Sonoma, Inc.: Creamy Tortellini Salad, Crunchy Coated Chicken Breasts, Chocolate Cupcake Cones, and Creamy Frosting.

From *Tom Douglas' Seattle Kitchen* by Tom Douglas (William Morrow & Co., 2000) © 2000 by Tom Douglas: Etta's Pit-Roasted Salmon with Grilled Shiitake Relish, Etta's Cornbread Pudding, Dahlia Pear Tart with Caramel Sauce, Star Anise Game Hens, Crispy Sesame Rice Cakes, Triple Coconut Cream Pie, and Coconut Pie Shell.

From *Lauren Groveman's Kitchen: Nurturing Food for Family and Friends* by Lauren Groveman (Chronicle Books, 1994) © 1994 by Lauren Groveman: Challah, Sandwich Loaf, and Raisin Loaves with Cinnamon Swirl.

From *How to Cook without a Book* by Pam Anderson (Broadway Books, 2000) © 2000 by Pam Anderson: Weeknight Stir-Fry, Stir-Fried Chicken with Baby Corn and Zucchini, Stir-Fried Chicken, Snow Peas, and Water Chestnuts, Stir-Fried Beef with Celery and Water Chestnuts, Lemon Flavoring Sauce, Sweet-and-Sour Flavoring Sauce, Basil (or Cilantro) Flavoring Sauce, Soy-Sesame Flavoring Sauce, Seared Salmon Fillets, Sautéed Boneless, Skinless Chicken Cutlets, Lemon-Caper Pan Sauce, Orange-Dijon Pan Sauce with Rosemary, Curried Chutney Pan Sauce, and Steamed/Sautéed Vegetables.

From *Sweet Miniatures: The Art of Making Bite-Size Desserts* by Flo Braker (Chronicle Books, 1991) © 1991 by Flo Braker: Sweet Cheese Puffs, Harlequins, and Chocolate Cherry Chaps.

From *Biba's Taste of Italy* by Biba Caggiano (HarperCollins Publishers, 2001) © 2001 by Biba Caggiano: Pork Loin Braised in Milk (Arrosto di Maiale nel Latte), Oven-Roasted Stuffed Vegetables (Verdure Ripiene al Forno), Fried Flatbread Fritters (Gnocco Fritto Modenese), Roasted Stuffed Turkey Breast (Arrosto di Tacchino Farcito), Sweet-and-Sour Onions with Balsamic Vinegar (Cipolline in Agrodolce), and Ricotta Gnocchi with Proscuitto and Porcini Mushroom Sauce (Gnocchi con Sugo di Prosciutto e Funghi Porcini).

From *Saveur Cooks Authentic Italian: Savoring the Recipes and Traditions of the World's Favorite Cuisine* by the Editors of *Saveur* Magazine (Chronicle Books, 2001) © 2001 by Meigher Communications, L.P.: Tagliata di Manzo (Sliced Grilled Steak), Minestrone Genovese (Genoese Vegetable Soup), and Bruschetta (Grilled Bread with Olive Oil and Garlic).

From *50 Chowders: One-Pot Meals—Clam, Corn & Beyond* by Jasper White (Scribner & Son, 2000) © 2000 by Jasper White: Pacific Northwest Salmon Chowder, Traditional Fish Stock, and Sweet Corn Fritters.

From Jasper White: Scallops and Bacon Skewers with Maple-Lemon Glaze.

From *The Thanksgiving Table: Recipes and Ideas to Create Your Own Holiday Tradition* by Diane Morgan (Chronicle Books, 2001) © 2001 by Diane Morgan: Butter-Rubbed Roast Turkey with an Apple Cider Glaze, Brined Turkey, Apple Cider Brine, Bread Stuffing with Apples, Bacon, and Caramelized Onions, and Gratin of Fennel and Tomato.

From *Healthy 1 - 2 - 3: The Ultimate 3 Ingredient Cookbook* by Rozanne Gold (Stewart Tabori & Chang, 2001) © 2001 by Rozanne Gold: Sautéed Chicken Breasts with Oven-Dried Grapes, Roasted Asparagus and Orange Salad, Asparagus "Fettuccine," and Lacquered Salmon, Pineapple-Soy Reduction.

From *The '21' Cookbook: Recipes and Lore from New York's Fabled Restaurant* by Michael Lomonaco with Donna Forsman (Doubleday, 1995) © 1995 by Michael Lomonaco: Pasta with Sundried Tomatoes and Mushrooms.

From Michael Lomonaco: Panfried Catskill Trout with Wild Mushrooms and Asparagus, and Warm Goat Cheese and Beet Salad.

From *Weber's Big Book of Grilling* by Jamie Purviance and Sandra S. McRae (Chronicle Books, 2001) © 2001 by Jamie Purviance and Sandra S. McRae: Yakitori Chicken, Strawberries Balsamico, Madras-Style Meatball Kebabs, and Swordfish Kebabs with Pasta Provençal.

Lauren Groveman, host of Home Cooking

Acknowledgments

When the idea for *Home Cooking* was just an idea on paper, the folks at KitchenAid immediately saw the potential of bringing, through national television, the best culinary experts into people's homes on a weekly basis. After all, even the best appliances need good cooking skills and great recipes to go along with them. Now, with four successful seasons on the air, KitchenAid continues to support *Home Cooking* and the diverse group of talented authors it features. We owe a great deal of thanks to Brian Maynard, who has supported the project in countless ways with his leadership and vision, not to mention his tremendous knowledge of cooking.

We'd also like to thank our hardworking, vivacious, and energetic host, Lauren Groveman, who graciously welcomed all the *Home Cooking* guests into the set kitchen, asking insightful questions and making them feel comfortable. We were also fortunate to have Shirley Corriher as a regular guest. Besides having tremendous talents as a cookbook author, she is a leading food scientist who has the answer to just about any cooking problem. Kevin Zraly, our Windows on the World wine guru, was another regular guest on the program. His ability to make wine comprehensible and fun is unparalleled.

The beautiful *Home Cooking* kitchen set was provided to us courtesy of Wood-Mode, manufacturers of kitchen cabinetry. Their craftsmanship, attention to detail, and superb quality made it a dream kitchen. A big thank-you also to Avonite, who supplied us with their innovative, solid surface countertops for the set, made from their attractive stonelike material. We were also very fortunate to have the participation of Kohler, whose outstanding faucets are not only beautiful, but also a real pleasure to work with. And finally to the company whose name has become synonymous with grilling—Weber. We are very grateful to them for providing us with one of their extraordinary Summit gas grills, which so many of our cookbook authors enjoyed using.

We'd like to thank Isabelle von Boch from Villeroy & Boch for providing us with their beautiful dinnerware to use on the programs. Similarly, a big thank-you to Frances Gravely from Vietri, the Italian ceramics company, for letting us use so many of their exquisite pieces. We are also very grateful to Eschenbach Porcelain for providing so many of their beautiful plates to us.

—Marjorie Poore and Alec Fatalevich

KitchenAid

A Humble Beginning

The modern KitchenAid stand mixer began with a single drop of sweat off the end of a busy baker's nose. The year was 1908 and Herbert Johnston, an engineer and later President of the Hobart Manufacturing Company in Troy, Ohio, was watching the baker mix bread dough with an age-old iron spoon. To help ease that burden, Johnston pioneered the development of an 80-quart mixer. By 1915 professional bakers had an easier, more thorough, and more sanitary way of mixing their wares.

In fact, that amazing, labor-saving machine caught on so quickly, the United States Navy ordered the Hobart mixers for its three new battleships, the *California, Tennessee,* and *South Carolina.* By 1917 the mixer was classified as "regular equipment" on all U.S. Navy ships.

The success of the commercial mixer gave Hobart engineers inspiration to create a mixer suitable for the home, but World War I interfered and the concept of a home mixer was put on hold.

1919—The Birth of Kitchen Icon

The year 1919 was truly a time of change. The gray days of war were giving way to the gaiety of the Roaring 20s. The spark of women's suffrage had ignited and women across America would soon earn the right to vote. America was on the brink of an era of peace and prosperity.

While factories across the country were busily converting to peacetime production, a small manufacturing company in a sleepy, southwest Ohio town revived its effort to design the first electrical "food preparer" for home use.

The first home stand mixer was born in 1919 at the Troy Metal Products Company, a subsidiary of the Hobart Manufacturing Company. The descendant of the large commercial food mixers, the Model H-5 was the first in a long line of quality home food preparers utilizing a revo-lutionary mixing system the company called "planetary action." This unique KitchenAid system, in which the beater rotates in one direction while moving it around the bowl in the opposite direction, is used in KitchenAid mixers today.

Another unique feature of the original that is found in today's stand mixer is the hub, which makes it possible to increase the mixer's versatility with a variety of attachments, including, among others, a food grinder, pasta maker, and fruit and vegetable juicers. Attachments are fully interchangeable for use with any model; even those designed for use with the first KitchenAid home mixer can be used with today's models.

Wives of Troy executives tested the initial prototypes. While discussing possible names for the new machine, one homemaker commented, "I don't care what you call it, but I know it's the best kitchen aid I have ever had!" A brand name was born and the first KitchenAid stand mixer was introduced to the American consumer.

The KitchenAid H-5 rolled off the newly founded KitchenAid Manufacturing Company's assembly line at the rate of four per day and was priced at $189.50. The overriding concern then, as now: Every KitchenAid mixer produced must be of unsurpassed quality so every unit was tested and retested. That same thorough testing goes on today just down the road from Troy at the Greenville plant, where KitchenAid mixers have been built by generations of dedicated workers for more than fifty years.

When retailers were reluctant to sell the unique "food preparer," KitchenAid set out to sell the mixers door-to-door using a largely female sales force (strong enough to carry the 65-lb. Model H-5 on sales calls). Homemakers were encouraged to invite friends to their homes, where the KitchenAid salesperson would prepare food for the group showcasing the new stand mixer. By the 1930s the KitchenAid mixer had earned wide acceptance and dealers began to show interest.

Meeting Consumers' Needs

1920s

As early as 1923 the KitchenAid mixer was promoted in national magazines such as *Good Housekeeping* and *The Saturday Evening Post*. This exposure acquainted millions of Americans with this revolutionary product and informed them of its capabilities.

In the mid-1920s production had increased to five mixers per day, which was considered excellent efficiency. The price was now $150 (approximately $1,500 in today's dollars), with an easy payment plan offered.

By the late 1920s American kitchens were growing smaller. KitchenAid responded with a smaller, lighter stand mixer at a lower price. The Model G proved so popular that Model H-5 was discontinued.

1930s

The 1930s brought the Depression and with it, rising unemployment. The Model G was beyond the means of most Americans. KitchenAid confronted the problem, recruiting Egmont Arens, a nationally acclaimed editor and world-renowned designer, to develop new stand mixer models. Within three years KitchenAid introduced three less expensive models that were within the means of many American households. The Model K, first introduced in 1937, was more compact than the G and moderately priced at $55. The Arens designs were of such timeless simplicity and functionality that they remain virtually unchanged to this day.

By the late 1930s demand for KitchenAid stand mixers was so great that the factory sold out before Christmas each year. But in 1941 World War II intervened and the plant converted to the production of munitions.

The Post War Years

During the war years production of KitchenAid stand mixers was limited. As peace arrived and the troops came home, production of KitchenAid stand mixers began again in earnest. KitchenAid moved to expanded facilities in Greenville, Ohio, and increased production. Dedicated Greenville employees continue to produce KitchenAid countertop appliances in these facilities today. KitchenAid, always in the forefront of trends, introduced daring new colors at the 1955 Atlantic City Housewares Show. These colors—Petal Pink, Sunny Yellow, Island Green, Satin Chrome, and Antique Copper—were a bold departure from the white appliances standard at the time. To this day KitchenAid countertop appliances are available in a variety of decorator colors as well as classic white.

The KitchenAid Dishwasher—Another Success Story

In 1926, Hobart acquired Crescent Washing Machine. In the Crescent product lineup was a commercial dishwasher, a descendant of the automatic dishwashing device introduced by inventor Josephine Cochrane at Chicago's 1893 Columbian Exposition. Hobart engineers began work on a home dishwasher but were interrupted by World War II. At last, in 1948, the KitchenAid home dishwasher made its debut at the National Housewares Exhibit. American homemakers enthusiastically welcomed its outstanding convenience, performance, and dependability. The growth of the dishwasher's popularity was impressive. As demand grew, marketing activities grew also. In 1954 a KitchenAid dishwasher display room was set up at Chicago's famed Merchandise Mart.

As more and more women joined the American workforce, the demand for time- and laborsaving appliances increased and homemakers who associated the KitchenAid name with quality and dependability wanted more KitchenAid appliances to help them manage their households. The success of the dishwasher led in short order to the introduction of KitchenAid built-in ovens and cooktops, food waste disposers, trash compactors, and hot water dispensers.

Today—Everything for the Well-Equipped Kitchen

In 1986 a full line of KitchenAid major appliances, including dishwashers, freestanding and built-in electric and gas cooking products, freestanding refrigerators, and laundry appliances, was introduced. Built-in refrigerators followed soon after in response to consumer demand for KitchenAid styling and performance in an increasingly popular appliance.

The 1990s saw the KitchenAid stand mixer joined by a succession of products that have become kitchen necessities, including hand mixers, blenders, food processors, toasters, and coffee makers. The introduction of cookware in 1999 and cutlery in 2000 rounded out the lineup of premium quality products in the KitchenAid Collection.

Today, the legacy of quality established in 1919 lives on not only in the multifunctional stand mixer, but also in a full line of kitchen appliances and culinary products sold across the world. Every product that carries the KitchenAid name, whether purchased in Paris or Peoria, carries a guarantee of outstanding performance, reliability, and versatility. A guarantee that is backed by more than eighty years of excellence.

The distinctive silhouette of KitchenAid appliances can be seen in some of America's most famous home and restaurant kitchens. *Home Cooking,* which KitchenAid is proud to sponsor as part of an ongoing commitment to nurturing the talents of home chefs, marks the latest of many television cooking shows that have relied on KitchenAid appliances to perform faultlessly. Television viewers often see KitchenAid products in sitcom kitchens. Finding a top restaurant without at least one hardworking KitchenAid stand mixer is a real challenge.

Even museums, the ultimate showcase for design excellence, display KitchenAid products. San Francisco's avant-garde Museum of Modern Art has featured the KitchenAid stand mixer in an exhibit of American icons. The esteemed collection of the Smithsonian Institution includes a KitchenAid stand mixer.

From its humble beginnings among the cornfields of southwest Ohio, the name KitchenAid has become synonymous with quality. Although over the years KitchenAid has streamlined and updated designs and technology, its worldwide success can be traced to the solid foundation laid way back in 1919.

NOTES

_____

_____

_____

_____

_____

_____

_____

NOTES

_____

_____

_____

_____

_____

_____

_____